THE SEENAGER SCRIBBLES

ON TEENAGER TRENDS

NEERJA SINGH

INDIA · SINGAPORE · MALAYSIA

ISBN 979-8-89233-854-7

Contents

The Witch Renaissance

Remember "Sabrina the Teenager Witch"? It is an American TV sitcom based on the Archie Comics that premiered in 1996.

Who would have known that the wickedly funny and recklessly brave Sabrina in fact, heralded the Witch Renaissance we are seeing today?

Our GenNext women are turning to occult, they are pouring over astrology, crystals and tarot. Are the marketers, policymakers and leaders paying attention to the mainstreaming of "Professional Witches"?

Consider the possible reasons. Our young feel disenfranchised. The recent events have shaken the foundations of society. The Gen-past does not inspire confidence. Instability is on the rise. The usual channels do not seem to work.

In contrast, covens present an alternative to patriarchal hierarchies. There has been a rebranding of witches from wicked devil-worshippers to intuitive wisewomen. Witchcraft offers a vocabulary of exploration without being dogmatic and prescriptive. It is being described as a feminine-centred, earth-centred way of living. And there is choice! You could be a sea witch, kitchen witch, influencer witch with your own recipes for moon water and potions to manifest your desires.

This subculture is integrating youth, gender, creative, and digital culture. It is also being seen as a rational response to climatic devastation and gender revolution. And there is help from the web! It is as though Witchcraft was made for the internet. Digital witch-celebrities like @bloodmilk, @nonalimmen, and @_spirits flourish on Instagram, with tens of thousands of followers.

Perhaps the time is ripe for a female dominated, nature intensive revolution. The question to ask would be: is this a backlash against the scientific spirit of enlightenment that brought mankind to what we call "progress" today?

The Mental Health Advocacy

Social media has emerged as a powerful vehicle for mental health advocacy within Gen Z. Platforms like Instagram, TikTok, and Twitter have become spaces where individuals share their personal experiences with mental health challenges, offer support to others, and disseminate valuable information. Through hashtags, campaigns, and informative content, Gen Z is leveraging the reach of social media to raise awareness and create a sense of community around mental health.

In addition to online platforms, Gen Z is bringing mental health discussions into everyday conversations. This generation is normalizing the dialogue around mental well-being, encouraging open communication in schools, workplaces, and social circles. By openly discussing their struggles and triumphs, Gen Z is dismantling the barriers that have historically prevented individuals from seeking help or sharing their experiences.

Furthermore, Gen Z's advocacy extends beyond personal narratives to include systemic change. This generation recognizes the need for improved mental health support structures and is actively pushing for more accessible mental health resources in educational institutions and workplaces. Activism, campaigns, and lobbying efforts aim to destigmatize seeking help for mental health issues and ensure that mental health is prioritized in public policy.

The rise of mental health advocacy within Gen Z is indicative of a generation that places a premium on holistic well-being. By fostering a culture of empathy, understanding, and support, Gen Z is reshaping societal attitudes towards mental health, creating a more inclusive and compassionate environment for individuals navigating their mental health journeys. This movement signifies not only a commitment to individual well-being but also a collective effort to create a world where mental health is prioritized and destigmatized.

The True Generation

A dork used to be "a contemptible, odd, unstylish and socially awkward person".

Well, Gen Z (born 1997-2015) has redefined it to mean "a person who is unfashionable or socially awkward in a way regarded as appealing or cute."

In other words, Gen Z is embracing themselves just as they are.

And of course, the market is responding!

Clearasil has made note of the "acne positivity" movement on Instagram. They have hurriedly ditched their usual crystal-clear skin for the real raw pimpled face to sell their product.

This is the novel trend in consumer branding: one that is dorkily awkward and adorably real. ADORKABLE.

The formula includes a visually jarring aesthetic with a genuine, real life emotional appeal. Interestingly enough, it is not the system that the adorkables are looking to smash. They just want it repackaged for a quirky and suspicious new generation.

And it is not as though Gen Z's values like tolerance, justice, ecology are new, the difference is in where the gaze is directed.

While my generation strived for picture-perfection, GenX for public self-validation, Millennials for self-actualization, Gen Z wants personal self-expression, thank you very much!

The Generational Journey Analytics

You will score low on customer/client experience if your engagement strategy does not address generational differences.

Let's talk digital marketing skills.

By now, privacy and relevance are old buzzwords. How about customizations? That too. Well then, the meat of the matter is in "AI based custom algorithms".

My Dad thinks the computer never lies! When stuck, he says, "Ask the computer!"

I know what my generation wants. A predictable and uniform and easy to understand online experience.

But seenagers and teenagers? Oh, give us surprises, catch us off-guard and prepare to be rejected if your novelty does match up to our expectations.

India is a pretty paradox today. One of the world's oldest living civilizations is home to the world's largest youth population.

But marketers, don't be fooled. This hyper-competitive, price-sensitive, culturally-diverse market now poses the new challenge of generational differences in expectations. With the physical and digital worlds coupling, it is the customer journeys that will differentiate one brand from another.

How personalised, relevant and compelling is the hybrid AI user experience you offer the new generations ?

What is your Gen Z journey analytics saying?

The Virtual Fashion Shows

Gen Z is playing a transformative role in the fashion industry by championing and actively participating in the evolution of virtual fashion shows. This generation, born into a digital era, seamlessly blends technology and fashion, pushing the boundaries of traditional runway events.

Virtual fashion shows offer Gen Z a platform to express their creativity and challenge conventional norms. This tech-savvy generation embraces digital avatars, virtual environments, and augmented reality to curate immersive fashion experiences. By participating in and promoting virtual fashion shows, Gen Z is reshaping the narrative of what constitutes a fashion event, breaking away from the constraints of physical spaces.

Social media, particularly platforms like Instagram, TikTok, and Snapchat, serves as a stage for Gen Z to showcase their curated virtual fashion exhibits. The viral nature of content on these platforms allows fashion enthusiasts to rapidly share and engage with virtual runway experiences, fostering a global community that transcends geographical boundaries.

Gen Z's role extends beyond being mere spectators; they actively contribute to the democratization of fashion. Virtual fashion shows empower individuals to explore and experiment with their unique styles, irrespective of their physical location or access to traditional fashion capitals. This inclusivity aligns with Gen Z's values of diversity and self-expression.

Moreover, the environmental consciousness inherent in Gen Z is reflected in their support for virtual fashion shows. By embracing digital alternatives, they contribute to reducing the carbon footprint associated with traditional fashion events, addressing concerns about sustainability and environmental impact.

As influencers and content creators, Gen Z leverages virtual fashion shows to redefine beauty standards and challenge the industry's norms. By curating digital personas and engaging in avant-garde fashion presentations, they foster a more inclusive and imaginative representation of style.

In essence, Gen Z's role in virtual fashion shows is characterized by innovation, inclusivity, and a seamless fusion of technology and fashion. By embracing and driving the evolution of virtual fashion experiences, this generation is shaping the future of the industry, emphasizing creativity, accessibility, and sustainability in the process.

The Generational Independence

It is not just the young that are always the social change makers.

India's elderly people for instance, are moving with speed, in time and culture. They are driving change by choosing or being forced to choose generational independence and individualism.

Intergenerational reciprocity and mutual interdependence used to be a core value in Indian society. And even though Indian elders often spoke of not wishing to be undue "burdens" on their children and hoping to die "while [their] hands and feet are still working" not many foresaw it becoming a literal reality.

But India's seniors face a new terrain today. Having sent their children to elite schools, emphasising self-empowerment to the daughter as much as to the son, funding their studies abroad, they now find their families dispersed around the nation and globe. Interestingly, it is not that they have been passively left behind by their children. In many cases, they have pro-actively created new community models of living for themselves.

Many feel that their living separate from their adult children in Assisted Senior Living homes gives the younger generation, daughters-in-law particularly more freedom.

It relieves family stress and allows children to focus on moving up in life. It is also less lonely and convenient than managing one's own establishment.

This brand of generational independent living by choice, gives a lie to the dominant assumption that the elders are merely passive objects and incapable of personal agency, critical reflection and change. When aging and eldercare shifts from family to the self-reliant individual and extra-family institutions, you have a new form of senior personhood.

By extrapolation, social revolutions don't just happen when the young rework "old stuff" but also when the old folks meet "new stuff". Whether by choice or not is another story!

The Generational Business Ethics

How do you embed business ethics among a multi-generational workforce to build a culture of values?

Generations come with their idiosyncrasies and assumptions and personalities. The challenge is in being prepared for the newest generation without overlooking the highly skilled and experienced older cohort.

There was the command-and-control style of leadership. (Born 1922-45)

There is the live-to-work approach. (Born 1946-1964)

Then along came work-to-live philosophy. (Born 1965-82)

Enter the parents' darling-digital-natives. (Born 1983-2004)

Welcome next, the true-inclusive-clicktivism. (Born 1996-2015)

How do these generational themes affect the ethical health of organizations? Do the generations feel different degrees of pressure to compromise standards? Is there a relative rate of misconduct? Do the cohorts respond differently when reported? How do different generations resolve moral dilemmas?

While the older generations are sure to be excited at the "Code of Ethics", the younger workers may use social interaction and help mechanisms to seek advice.

There are ways to communicate a consistent core message to different generations. For the young, culture is the sum total of their interactions with co-workers but for the older lot, it is about stated values, top-down messages and their own beliefs about the company.

An effective ethics programme and a deep-rooted ethics culture that talks to all generations will attract, inspire and retain talent from each age group.

Gen Z, with their acute sensitivity to social equity and ecological balance and tech-savvy networking smarts may make great ethics ambassadors. But then they would be seen as lacking the integrity track record of the senior lot. A team-up would therefore, hit the bull's eye.

The magic key is in working and learning together.

The Political Activism on Social Media

Generation Z has harnessed the power of social media as a potent tool for political activism, leveraging online platforms to organize movements, raise awareness about social issues, and effect change on a global scale. This generation, known for its digital fluency and social consciousness, recognizes the potential of social media as a democratizing force that amplifies voices and accelerates the dissemination of information.

One of the key strengths of political activism on social media lies in its ability to facilitate the rapid spread of information. Gen Z utilizes platforms such as Twitter, Instagram, and TikTok to share news, engage in discussions, and raise awareness about critical social and political issues. Hashtags and trending topics become rallying points, allowing individuals to unite around common causes and generate momentum for movements.

Social media platforms serve as dynamic spaces for organizing and mobilizing political activism. Gen Z has demonstrated a remarkable capacity to coordinate and execute large-scale movements, from climate strikes to anti-racism protests. Online activism extends beyond geographic boundaries, enabling individuals worldwide to unite in solidarity, share resources, and collectively advocate for social change.

Moreover, social media provides a platform for marginalized voices to be heard. Activists within Gen Z use these platforms to highlight issues of social injustice, systemic inequality, and human rights abuses. The visual and narrative power of social media allows individuals to share personal stories, humanizing complex issues and fostering empathy among a global audience.

The impact of political activism on social media extends beyond virtual spaces. Gen Z's online advocacy often translates into offline action, with movements gaining traction and influencing policy decisions. Social media activism becomes a catalyst for real-world change as individuals mobilize their communities and connect with like-minded activists.

In conclusion, political activism on social media has become an integral aspect of Gen Z's approach to social change. The digital realm serves as a democratizing force, empowering individuals to raise their voices, organize movements, and effect meaningful change on a global scale. As this generation continues to navigate the digital landscape, its commitment to leveraging social media for political activism is shaping the future of social and political discourse.

Gen Z is at the forefront of a transformative movement: the rise of mental health advocacy. Unlike previous generations, Gen Z is actively dismantling the long-standing stigma surrounding mental health, fostering open conversations, and promoting mental well-being through various platforms.

The TikTok Resumes

Have you posted yours yet? It takes just 60 seconds. Use a green screen. Tell the camera why you deserve to be hired. Have your past experience flash behind you and in seconds viewers will tag potential employers.

tiktokresumes.com offers pro-tips from creators@ careerbabe and @wonsulting, among others.

Please don't tell me you are still labouring over your ONE PAGER! That is going the way of the overhead projectors and pagers and VHS tapes.

Oh please, you seriously need some inspo! Particularly when flying cars, clones, and colonies on other planets are fast approaching.

Gen Z job hunters are on the prowl, and it looks like the labour starved companies are interested. All it takes is a hashtag, contact information and their LinkedIn profile, by choice. Set the view to public and wait for the interviewer call!

Like with everything else though, there are concerns. Not everybody is a great content creator. Nor does everybody have screen presence. Not everybody may be skilled at search engine optimisation.

Maybe it is time to accept that life is unequal essentially. And that "follow your passion" was the cruellest scam unleashed on mankind since the idea of genetic superiority.

And just so you are wondering, all generations are eligible to submit TikTok résumés, age is no bar.

It just seems such a natural extension to the way we are communicating today, via videos and photos. It displays the skills-in-demand live.

So, there you have it. The new generations have found a way to leverage their strength while the old generations get to do panel discussions around a possibly biased algorithm.

Build Gen-bridges instead, with the Seenager!

The Boomer Parents

Increasingly, it would seem that some millennials and Gen Zs want little or nothing to do with their parents. It is the new-generation phenomenon of parental alienation or estrangement.

Not all parents drive their adult kids away however, with neglect or abuse. Some are being cast aside for reasons hard to understand. One hears of the children wanting to go "no contact" so as to escape "helicopter parenting" and work on their "co-dependency" issues. There are young woman running for cover from their "narcissistic mother's anxious voice".

This trend varies in degree from one culture to another. While in the USA, it may not be expected of a grown son to pay for his father's old age care, it has been somewhat of a tradition in India. In 2013, China's "Elderly Rights Law" prescribed it a crime not to visit your ageing parents.

Amongst the reasons, one is the "liquid nature" of society today where the normal has become obsolete. Parental connections stemmed from a sense of duty and obedience once, they now depend on how the parents make their kids feel about themselves. Is the relationship stressing the adult children, restricting their potential, curbing their individuality, guilting them?

The new generations are meeting their adulting markers later today and even when they do find a job and a life-partner, there is no saying! What then is left for them to do is to focus on their own development and pursuit of happiness.

Many young people feel they are treated like the "black sheep" of the family, constantly "gaslit", urged to "grow up", derided for being "too sensitive", dismissed for being "in pain". Parents on the other hand contest this, claiming that they put their heart and soul and life's blood into bringing up their kids: "what did they lack for" and "we attended parent training, read books" and "we were present at their special events" and "we put their health and well-being first".

There is a clear generational divide over who to permit into or thrown out of our lives and it is the therapists who provide these decisions a moral legitimacy. What was once considered expected forms of stress or suffering are today pathologized in psychiatric diagnosis. A highly involved parent could be considered "incestuous" for instance.

We are in a socio-cultural quicksand. The institutional constraints have long gone. We are free of the commitments that kept us anchored. It used to be about the clan and being in it together. From there we moved to blaming the government for everything. But in the modern narrative of individuality, personal choice and self-love, parents are being blamed for outcomes that may in fact be dependent on social status, genes, peer pressure, neighbourhood or just plain lady luck.

The Second Space Age

The Apollo and the Space Shuttle inspired the older generations, the millennials take inspiration from the superstar of the commercial space industry "SpaceX.'

Welcome all, to the shift from a space-for-earth economy (telecommunications and internet infrastructure, earth observation capabilities, national security satellites) to the space-for-space economy (mining the Moon or asteroids for material with which to construct in-space habitats or supply refuelling depots).

Until now, there were never more than 13 people at any given time in space, soon that could be hundreds, thousands, even millions of merry folks living in space.

There clearly has never been a better time to work in the space industry. In this new era of spaceflight led by private sector, millennials have far greater opportunities than the former space veterans. And they are girding up to launch us into space in a sustainable fashion and at scales.

What are the options being considered? Back to the Moon? The Moon as a steppingstone to Mars? Non-stop to Mars?

Back in the 60s, space exploration was about politics and national prestige. Today it is about money yes, but it is also to find ways to make the world a better place.

There is optimism, hope, adaptability, futuristic long-term thinking, and a desire to take everyone along on the ride.

The National Space Society (NSS) vision of "people living and working in thriving communities beyond the Earth, and the use of the vast resources of space for the dramatic betterment of humanity" seems merely some policies away from being realized.

There are serious implications here for business, policy, and society at large. Will Earthlings catch this bus?

The TikTok Challenges

TikTok challenges have transcended mere entertainment, evolving into a powerful medium through which Generation Z addresses social issues, advocates for change, and promotes inclusivity. This short-form video platform has become a dynamic space for cultural influence, fostering a sense of community and encouraging dialogue on topics ranging from activism to self-expression.

One of the notable aspects of TikTok challenges is their ability to amplify social issues and promote awareness. Hashtags associated with challenges often carry meaningful messages, serving as a rallying point for users passionate about specific causes. Whether it's raising awareness about environmental concerns, addressing mental health stigmas, or advocating for social justice, TikTok challenges provide a platform for individuals to share their perspectives and mobilize collective action.

Moreover, TikTok challenges play a crucial role in fostering inclusivity and celebrating diversity. Challenges centred around body positivity, LGBTQ+ representation, and cultural appreciation allow users to express themselves authentically and contribute to a more accepting digital environment. By participating in these challenges, individuals can challenge traditional beauty standards, break down stereotypes, and amplify underrepresented voices.

The global reach of TikTok challenges contributes to their cultural impact, making them a conduit for sharing diverse experiences and perspectives. The platform's algorithmic nature ensures that challenges have the potential to go viral, reaching audiences far beyond individual social circles. This broad dissemination of content fosters a sense of interconnectedness among users worldwide, contributing to the creation of a global community that transcends geographic and cultural boundaries.

TikTok challenges also act as a source of inspiration and creativity. Users engage with challenges by putting their unique spin on trends, adding personal touches, and contributing to the evolution of the challenge over time. This collaborative and iterative process fosters a culture of creativity and innovation within the TikTok community.

In essence, TikTok challenges have become a multifaceted phenomenon within Generation Z, serving as a platform for entertainment, activism, and cultural celebration. Through these challenges, individuals not only entertain but also educate, advocate, and connect on a global scale, shaping a digital landscape that reflects the values and aspirations of a generation committed to positive change.

The Idea of Friendship

How could friendship have evolved across generations when the cult sitcom "FRIENDS" created by boomers, featuring Gen Xers, internalized by the Millennials is now being binged upon by Gen Z?

The recent global study on friendship by SNAPCHAT covered nine nations, including India and the four main generations: Gen Z, born 1996-2012 (aged 13-23); Millennials, born 1979-1995 (aged 24-39); Gen X, born 1965-1979 (aged 40-54); and Boomers, born 1944-1964 (aged 55-75).

The questions were: Do the generations have the same average number of best friends? How different are their meeting spaces? What do they talk about? What do they value in close friends and what would they want to change?

Predictably, there was unanimous preference for emojis, photos and videos.

Interestingly however, the social platforms seem to have influenced generational perspectives on friendship. For the Facebook Millennials, it had become about the networks radiating from their immediate circles. But the TikTok and Snapchat Gen Zers are creating smaller groups.

There are other differences.

Millennials went to friends for open-minded and non-judgemental spaces but that trend also forced families to open up, in time for Gen Zs, who no longer seem to rely completely on friends to cushion youthful experiments,

While a degree of self-awareness in their close friend may be essential to the Millennial, for Gen Z it may boil down to who is making them feel good in that moment.

And although, instant responses on the social media project friendship to Gen Z, the Millennials may be less immediate, using technology to keep in touch or have life's difficult conversations.

But the one point this study failed to mention is the importance of low stakes connections IRL!

In real life, the number of friends will peak around mid-twenties, beginning to dwindle from then on as life takes over. What is sustainable however, is just being socially engaged.

Chatting with the dog-owner in the park. Exchanging greetings with your friendly car cleaner. Hobnobbing with the parent you meet at the school gate. Many of us don't consider these interactions worth our time anymore but it is this network of weak ties that can amplify our sense of well-being and happiness.

The Throwaway Culture

What key word today is the Brahmastra of inter-generational conflict?

It is Gen Zs new word 'cheugy,' pronounced "chew-gee."

Cheugy is a new insult targeting the uncool older people, in this case the Millennilas, the oldest of whom is touching 40 now.

Are you a bit off trend? You are a cheugy.

Skinny jeans, graphic t-shirts and low-top Converse? What a cheugy.

Don't be out of date or try too hard, that is cheaugy.

Slogan-wear and Statement-trainers are cheugy but Birkenstock sandals and Levi's jeans pass the test.

The older generations react by calling cheugy an ugly sounding and fake word with zero literary or linguistic merit. A stupid word to demean the uncool, they would have you know!

There is a marketing nuance here, however. As trending cycles pick up speed and attention spans go nano, the only way to avoid being called 'cheugy' is to constantly phase out your material possessions only to consume bigger, better and brighter products.

Overconsumption in other words and just what the corporations want.

How then to be un-cheugy?

Be thrifty. Make your own clothes. Look good for yourself and not for others. Create your own sense of style and buy things that are evergreen and classic, built to last.

Be like us boomers, we are sooooo un-cheugy!

The Cancel Culture Dynamics

Cancel culture has become a defining feature of Generation Z's social and digital landscape, reflecting a collective effort to hold individuals and brands accountable for controversial actions. This phenomenon, characterized by the public withdrawal of support and engagement, is driven by Gen Z's commitment to social justice, inclusivity, and a desire to enact change by leveraging the power of digital platforms.

Gen Z utilizes social media as a tool for activism, making cancel culture dynamics particularly prominent. When individuals or brands engage in actions perceived as offensive, harmful, or inconsistent with prevailing values, this generation mobilizes to express discontent and demand accountability. The mechanisms of cancel culture often include public condemnation, boycotts, and the withdrawal of support through unfollowing or disengaging from associated content.

Cancel culture serves as a form of collective accountability, emphasizing the responsibility of public figures and brands to align with societal expectations. This generation, known for its vocal stance on social issues, uses cancelling as a means to challenge power imbalances and demand accountability for actions that perpetuate discrimination, inequality, or harm.

The dynamics of cancel culture are also intertwined with a desire for authentic representation and cultural sensitivity. Gen Z scrutinizes not only the actions of individuals or brands but also the underlying values they project. Instances of cultural appropriation, insensitivity, or perpetuation of harmful stereotypes are met with swift and vocal backlash, reflecting a generation that values inclusivity and demands that public figures and brands align with these values.

While cancel culture has been effective in holding individuals and brands accountable, it is not without its criticisms. Some argue that it can lead to a lack of nuance and opportunities for growth and education. Nevertheless, for Gen Z, cancel culture is a tool for driving social change and promoting a more accountable and responsible digital culture.

The dynamics of cancel culture within Generation Z showcase a generation actively participating in shaping societal values through the digital sphere. It reflects a commitment to social justice, inclusivity, and a belief in the power of collective action to enforce accountability in an increasingly interconnected and influential digital landscape.

The Olympic Star

Name the real star at the Tokyo Olympics.

It is mental health.

Even the hearts watching on, are aching and breaking. There is at long last, acknowledgment of the pain, distress and anguish caused by decades of unquestioned litanies around being the most glorious, gritty and gladiator like.

Tom Dumoulin, Michael Phelps, Simone Biles, Naomi Osaka, Sha'Carri Richardson have sounded a clarion call for revision of assumptions that older generations have lived by.

Are we listening?

The term 'Olympic Champion' can be a burden. It is perfectly alright not to be 'perfect'. What is wrong with taking a break to clear the head? Having to use marijuana or medication to dull anxiety and pain before entering the sporting world stage is unacceptable.

But the heightened scrutiny and external expectations placed on the world's young athletes by the devices is breaking them. The uncertainty involved is too much to take.

It is heartening that psychologists and psychiatrists are stationed onsite in the Olympic village. There is a

"Mentally Fit Helpline" made available before, during and for three months after the Games. Medals are important but not at the cost of mental health.

The onus is on earlier generations to make mental health services available to the young.

Gen Z has named the elephant, loud and clear.

The Socially-Distanced App

There is a reason this socially distant app became a craze with Gen Z (born 1997-2012) during the lockdown.

Its 29-year-old creator @JoshuaLengfelder aimed to get people into "random exploration" beyond their "predetermined realities" including areas outside their regular conscious awareness. The idea was to have users step out of comfort zones, break rigidity, see new connections and disrupt boring routines. Also, get some exercise!

Randonautica, the app, asks users to set their radii and choose from spaces named 'attractors', 'voids', or 'anomalies'. It also suggests that they 'focus' their 'intent' in a mind matter interaction principle. Where the user goes is determined by a quantum random number generator (QRNGs).

People have been known to hit regular spaces like car parks, highways, water bodies but some others ended up in cemeteries, true life crime scenes and spooky haunts. There is a documented case of a group of teenagers being led by their Randonautica co-ordinates to discover a suitcase stuffed with remains of a body in Seattle.

Millions of gen-next are roaming random locations with Randonautica, hunting the hidden corners of reality. The app comes with warnings not to venture into the night or trespass or break the law but there have been cases of young people wandering into unfamiliar zones and videoing themselves in the process to share on TokTok.

Incredibly, the creator credits the synchronicities to some form of "quantum entanglement". He draws upon the work of the Princeton Engineering Anomalies Research (PEAR) programme that suggested that humans could, through 'micro-psychokinesis', influence a random number generator simply through their thoughts.

Imagine a Gen Z, tip-toeing home in the inky night, thinking his/her unconscious manifested his experience.

Please do not issue statements such as "Don't Go Randonauting!" You know what that will make Gen Z want to do!

The Gender Fluidity and Expression

In a powerful departure from traditional gender norms, Generation Z is at the forefront of challenging societal expectations and embracing gender fluidity as a fundamental aspect of identity and expression. This generation, known for its progressive views and commitment to social justice, is actively reshaping the discourse around gender, fostering a more inclusive understanding that goes beyond the confines of binary constructs.

Gen Z's approach to gender fluidity is characterized by a rejection of rigid gender norms and a celebration of diverse expressions of identity. This encompasses a spectrum of gender identities beyond the traditional binary, acknowledging that individuals may not fit neatly into categories of "male" or "female." The recognition and acceptance of non-binary, genderqueer, and gender non-conforming identities contribute to a more nuanced and inclusive understanding of gender.

Expression becomes a key element in Gen Z's approach to gender fluidity. This generation embraces the freedom to express oneself authentically, regardless of societal expectations tied to gender. Fashion choices, hairstyles, and overall presentation are seen as personal expressions of identity rather than rigid markers of masculinity or femininity. The breaking down of traditional gender-based fashion norms allow individuals to explore and experiment with their appearance in a way that aligns with their self-perception.

Social media plays a significant role in amplifying and normalizing gender fluidity. Gen Z utilizes platforms like Instagram, TikTok, and YouTube to share stories, challenges, and triumphs related to gender identity and expression. This digital space has become a powerful tool for community-building, fostering connections among individuals who share similar experiences and providing a platform for education and awareness.

The push for gender inclusivity within Gen Z is not just about personal identity but also extends to advocating for systemic change. This generation is vocal about the need for inclusive policies, education, and representation across various spheres, challenging institutions to adapt to a more nuanced understanding of gender.

In essence, Generation Z's approach to gender fluidity and expression is characterized by a commitment to dismantling traditional norms, fostering inclusivity, and embracing the complexity and diversity of human identity. As this generation continues to shape societal attitudes, it is contributing to a more open, accepting, and liberated understanding of gender for present and future generations.

The New Career Paths

There is an underlying assumption in Harvard's Advanced Leadership Initiative or Stanford's Distinguished Careers Institute.

The premise is that human lives see two distinct career phases. The first is ego-driven, self-oriented and profit-focused, the second is about giving back to society.

It does not hold true however, for many women. Their first half is spent balancing work, community, and family, it is only in the second half that they may discover their voices and dreams.

"It took me until 60 to discover that 'No' was a complete sentence," said Jane Fonda. That tribe is growing. Think Kristalina Georgieva, MD IMF or Angela Merkel, Chancellor Germany or Jane Fraser, Chief Executive of Citigroup.

So, relax millennial generation women! Your 30s are not your make-or-break years. Stay alive and kicking since you have decades to spread it over now. It is not that you can't have it all, "you can't have it all at the same time" in the words of Jane Fraser.

business leaders will have to create flexible work systems that serve employees best across the decades.

Peter Drucker's words have proved prophetic, "In future, there will almost certainly be two distinct workforces, broadly made up of the under 50s and the over 50s respectively. These two workforces are likely to differ markedly in their needs and behaviour, and in the jobs they do."

As a species, we will be seeing many more older humans in the future than ever before. What they do with their extra years will affect us all.

Fancy these new generational differences!

A mass of older men giving back and older women leading.

The Millennial Shadow Board

Have your young workers tuned you out? Does your Executive Board hit the right market vibes?

Well, Deloitte India and EY India have found the alternative to pulse surveys and town hall, it is called the “Shadow & Millennial Board” or the “NexCo”. Unconventional decision making, unfiltered views, pace with the dynamic environment...the new generation brings it all. Generational diversity is here to direct and drive business impact.

The “shadow board” is made up of talented non-executive employees that works with senior executives on strategic initiatives. They bring the tech wizardry, maverick marketing skills and that all important wake-up call.Airbnb reinvented their business model to Jo&Joe, the “urban shelter for Millennials” with the help of their free-spirited shadow board.

Stora Enso, the Finnish paper and packaging company, redesigned their processes by letting their shadow board assign some tasks to non-experts instead of the default experts.

GroupM India implemented a digital and cultural transformation with the help of their shadow board that also developed their social media platform called Yammer to facilitate conversations across agencies.

Shadow boards in return, work well to give the Millennials increased visibility, access, and eventual promotions.

Given that some of the most successful companies in the recent past have been creations of under-35s, it stands to reason that companies would want to take on these "wildcards" to help ready for the future.

Are closed doors passe? Have we embraced the revolution? Does succession planning have a new name? What do the older generations feel about this?

The Crypto Collectibles

In the fast-evolving digital landscape, non-fungible tokens (NFTs) have emerged as a captivating phenomenon, particularly for Generation Z. This generation, characterized by its tech-savviness and an inclination towards digital experiences, has embraced NFTs as a unique intersection of art, self-expression, and investment. The rise of crypto collectibles has redefined traditional notions of ownership and creativity, marking a significant cultural shift.

Crypto collectibles, often built on blockchain technology, are unique digital assets represented by NFTs. These tokens certify ownership and authenticity, making each item distinct and irreplaceable. Gen Z's embrace of crypto collectibles spans a wide range of digital assets, from digital art and virtual real estate to in-game items and other forms of digital content.

The allure of crypto collectibles for Gen Z lies in the opportunity for self-expression and personalization. NFTs allow individuals to own and showcase digital art and assets in a way that goes beyond traditional physical ownership. The digital nature of these collectibles aligns with a generation that values the virtual realm as a legitimate space for cultural and artistic expression.

Moreover, the investment potential of crypto collectibles has not gone unnoticed by Gen Z. The decentralized and transparent nature of blockchain technology provides a sense of security and authenticity in transactions, attracting individuals who see these digital assets as not only a form of self-expression but also a potential investment opportunity. The value of certain NFTs has surged, creating a new dimension in the world of digital assets and collectibles.

As Gen Z continues to explore the possibilities of crypto collectibles, the cultural and economic impact is becoming increasingly evident. From supporting digital artists to creating unique online identities, the rise of NFTs has opened new avenues for creative expression and financial engagement, shaping a digital landscape where ownership, creativity, and investment converge in novel and unprecedented ways.

The Online Class Raider

In order to kill boredom, the more enterprising of Gen Z have been ordering entertainment from a new class of service providers. It's the YouTuber specializing in "raiding" online classes and livestreaming them on Discord!

Discord as in the chat app boomers, not your English word for 'disagreement' here.

The SOP is simple. Send the Online Class Raider a link, ID and password to the scheduled class via a DM. Or give it away in a public comment on the social accounts of these raiders.

He might enter in fancy dress or crack a joke or sing a viral song or rap a poem or masquerade as a Zoom official.

The Raiders stack up hundreds of disrupted classes. Their subscriber counts shoot up.

Gen Z invites them to relieve the stress and pressures they are suffering during the pandemic. A few ask them to abuse their teachers! One raider claimed to be getting 300 to 500 such requests a day.

But like everything else, there is the flip side. Some of these raiders have had their channels hacked. They have been known to be disowned by the very kids who invited them. Screenshots of female students have been photoshopped for memes.

Some of this may spring from angst at too much strictness or slow data speed or having to share the smartphone or teachers being casual enough to cook during classes or schools charging fee for transport during lockdown.

What is worrisome is that many Gen Zers do not realize that Zoom raiding amounts to criminal offence. The punishment can range from internal disciplinary action to 3 to 5 years in jail.

A raider's claim of just wanting to give the stressed children a few minutes of entertainment may transform unknowingly into stalking or privacy concerns.

Shweta Chawla, Digital Forensic Investigator, Head, SC Cyber Solutions says, "There have been instances where such miscreants have linked the attendees' names, IDs, and other details to escorts services as well. The class stops being a safe environment."

The AI-Human Economy

Dear Generation Z. Have you a sense of what you are up against? Machine intelligence will scale in your generation. You Gen Z, might be entirely disrupted by AI, machine learning and the rise of actual robots.

Work, consumerism, nature of money may alter in fundamental ways during your lifetimes. Code will soon write itself, tasks in QA testing automation will be care of machine intelligence and AI-as-a-service tools will render many a job obsolete.

If you want to compete with robots, you will have to focus on human connections.

As machines get more and more technically proficient, "soft" skills such as intellectual insight, flexibility, intuition, and creativity become the complementary arsenal.

The trick is to stand out from the robots! Your communication skills will build you better relationships and successful collaborations.

Remember that even though you are digitally proficient and multidimensional, your Microsoft Excel talent may have to interpret the data instead. Be prepared to upskill on a continuum.

Your ability to adapt to a rapidly robotizing work environment will decide your prosperity.

You could also find work that is a unique amalgam of your lived experiences and training to put yourself out of a robot's competitive radius.

Technological automation is accelerating and will completely disrupt and transform entire sectors of employment.

The promise of AI, however, belies the human cost involved. Should tech companies continue to grow unregulated, systems of governance and society will change beyond recognition.

You Gen Z have the choice of being the most innovative and humane generations of the 21st and 20th centuries. You must prepare to play your role in the AI-human economy of the future here.

The Inclusive Beauty Standards

Generation Z has emerged as a powerful force in reshaping beauty standards, demanding inclusivity and challenging the historically narrow and unrealistic ideals perpetuated by the beauty industry. This generation, marked by its commitment to diversity and social justice, is actively promoting a more inclusive representation that celebrates the richness of human beauty in all its forms.

Gen Z is pushing back against traditional beauty standards that have long been dominated by Eurocentric ideals, embracing a wide spectrum of skin tones, body shapes, and gender expressions. Social media platforms serve as powerful tools for this generation to amplify their voices and challenge the status quo, promoting the visibility of individuals who have historically been underrepresented in mainstream beauty narratives.

Inclusive beauty standards are about more than just representation; they encompass a call for authenticity and the celebration of individuality. Gen Z seeks to dismantle the notion that beauty is confined to a narrow set of characteristics and features. The embrace of imperfections, unique features, and diverse expressions of identity challenges the airbrushed and homogenized images that have permeated traditional beauty standards.

The beauty industry, in response to the demands of Gen Z, is gradually evolving. Brands are becoming more cognizant of the need for diverse representation in their marketing campaigns, product offerings, and influencer collaborations. The rise of beauty influencers who defy conventional standards and celebrate their authentic selves has also contributed to a more inclusive beauty landscape.

Moreover, Gen Z's advocacy for inclusive beauty standards extends beyond individual empowerment. It is a movement rooted in the belief that everyone deserves to feel seen, valued, and beautiful. By challenging the rigid norms that have defined beauty for so long, this generation is contributing to a cultural shift that celebrates diversity, fosters self-acceptance, and promotes a more inclusive and affirming beauty industry. In doing so, Gen Z is reshaping the conversation around beauty, making it a space that is truly reflective of the rich tapestry of human identity.

The Hacker University

A hacker university is selling cybercrime courses designed to hack for profit and commit fraud.

And of course, little or no coding experience is required.

HackTown is the name of the hacker university. The courses offered range from operational security to network attacks to Wi-Fi hacking and carding, to start with. One can then advance to skills aimed at accessing router admin panels, zeroing in on targets inside a compromised network, brute force attacks, man-in-the-middle attacks, deployment of ransomwares and remote access trojans (RATs). The university also boasts a resource shop stocked with malware, keyloggers, password stealers.

The professionalization of cybercrime is clearly keeping pace with the field of cybersecurity. In floundering economies, there is a real danger of cybercrime winning over a career in legitimate cybersecurity.

Alternative educational paths have thrown up this oxymoron "illegal but professional way".

Just as the global universities began to teach remotely, the cybercriminals jumped on, their task made easy with straightforward payment systems and content access such as exploits and proof of concept code. The YouTube Marketing Hacks is crawling with beginner level hacker information anyway, all that is needed is a pair of young, restless, and idle hands on the keyboard.

Young adults and teenagers are a target market for hacker universities.

To counteract this, perhaps a career in cybersecurity needs to be made more appealing and accessible.

At this time, the modern cybercrime industry is ahead in organizational efficiency. The reason? Unlike cyber start-ups that keep receiving venture funding even when losing money, the cybercriminals do not have the luxury of making mistakes.

The Indian Legacy

What legacy is the 75-year-old Indian democracy leaving behind for her next generation? Despite the huge odds against economic growth, social progress and human development.

From 799 Indian universities in 2015, the figure rose to 1,043 last year. The agricultural exports from India have soared to a record $19 billion, thank you MS Swaminathan. The nation is one of the world's largest dairy producers, thank you Verghese Kurien.

India became the first country to launch an interplanetary mission Mangalyaan successfully in its first attempt, thank you ISRO. India's lunar probe Chandrayaan 1 was launched successfully at a fraction of the cost of similar programmes of other countries. We are home to one of the six government agencies in the world with full-launch capabilities to deploy cryogenic engines, launch extra-terrestrial missions and operate large fleets of artificial intelligence satellites.

India's advanced atomic energy programme has a stellar safety and security record. We are the globe's largest supplier of low-cost generic medicines, with the second largest number of US Food and Drug Administration-approved manufacturing plants. India's IT industry accounts for approximately 55% of the global service sourcing market.

We host the world's third largest technology start-up ecosystem, with 11,000 to 12,500 start-ups incepted in 2015 to 2020. As of 2020, India has the third largest number of unicorns in the world. Our new generation is on the rise with the necessary skills and resources to both forge and cross frontiers.

Independence Day Greetings Country peeps! Thank you global community for showing us the mirror, collaborating and helping us as also keeping ourselves real.

The Minimalist Lifestyle

In a marked departure from the consumerist mindset of previous generations, Generation Z has embraced a minimalist lifestyle, redefining the parameters of success and contentment. This cohort, born into a world saturated with materialism and excess, is spearheading a cultural shift that prioritizes experiences over possessions, values intentional living, and seeks fulfilment beyond the accumulation of things.

At the core of the minimalist lifestyle is a rejection of the notion that happiness is intrinsically tied to material possessions. Gen Z, marked by a heightened environmental awareness and a desire for authenticity, challenges the status quo by consciously opting for a more streamlined existence. This rejection of excess is reflected in choices that prioritize quality over quantity, with an emphasis on possessions that hold genuine value and utility.

Experiences take precedence over material goods in the minimalist worldview. Gen Z places a premium on creating memories, fostering relationships, and engaging in activities that enrich their lives. Travel, cultural exploration, and shared moments with loved ones become the currency of a minimalist lifestyle, representing a departure from the conventional markers of success that were once defined by conspicuous consumption.

The minimalist ethos extends beyond personal choices and seeps into broader consumer behavior. Gen Z's inclination toward minimalism has significant implications for industries that have traditionally thrived on excess and constant consumption. Brands and businesses are now compelled to align with values that prioritize sustainability, ethical production, and products that serve a genuine purpose.

In the digital age, where the pursuit of perfection is often amplified through social media, the minimalist lifestyle emerges as a counter-cultural response. Gen Z embraces imperfections, values sustainability, and seeks joy in simplicity. This intentional living represents not only a rejection of materialism but also a conscious effort to contribute to a more sustainable and meaningful way of life, indicative of a generation redefining the metrics of success and fulfilment.

The Management Shift

For William Wordsworth's generation "Child is the father of man" meant that the personality we form as children endures into our adult life.

'Child is the father of man' however, is coming true in a literal sense today. The new generations head the shift in mass consciousness we are seeing around us. Take business and management schools. It used to be a dog-eat-dog world. At what point did social entrepreneurs steal up to take over as captains of the industry? One doesn't see this in other professions such as law or medicine where the framework, competencies and code of conduct are established and fairly synthesized. Management students by contrast, bring in their own worldview, lived experiences and social influences to create their reality on the campuses.

And that new air is one of cooperation, not competition. It is about evolving systems and not a rigid assumption of transgression. The new leader is no longer macho, he/she is egalitarian.

Does the business world acknowledge this re-evaluation? Is it keeping pace with the new purposes and roles? Given how different the social mood is against the generic meltdown, the new student will have to be accommodated with an updated curriculum. Will this delegitimization of swash-buckling leadership last? Who knows?

For now, the new generation management students are coming in with a ready ideal of their most admired CEOs. There is a representation of leadership they may have chosen to incorporate and emulate. Their own industrial experience coupled with the media stories define their personal discernments.

The talk is of teams working together. And the guiding spirit is group wisdom.

The Internet Shaming

The internet and social media have taken public shaming to a distressing level. The reasons for this shaming behaviour can range from infidelity to socially inappropriate behaviour to customer complaints to doxing to criminal behaviour to revenge to social justice and on it goes. There are special websites created for shamers to vent on each of these subjects.

While public shaming sites are easy to use, the punishing consequences of doing so are not appreciated well enough. Online shaming can ruin reputations and careers. It can cause severe psychological damage. The poster can be targeted in return. And there are civil and criminal lawsuits that can land.

A split-second decision to post something online can lead to a lifetime of pain and regret, for both the shamer and the victim. Shame can last forever on the internet today. It is next to impossible to take back a shaming post. And the momentary satisfaction of such a post is certainly not worth the storm that can follow.

How else may one address feelings of anger, frustration, or humiliation? There are more effective alternatives. The confrontation could be done in person for a sense of closure. Another way would be to walk away instead of escalating a negative situation. And there is always the legal action available by reporting a crime to the proper authorities.

The prevalence of online shaming is a matter of grave social concern. It is a thought that should be rethought more than twice.

The Educational Influencers

Generation Z has ushered in a new era of learning, characterized by a departure from traditional educational methods and a keen interest in seeking knowledge from unconventional sources. Educational influencers, particularly on platforms like YouTube, have become instrumental in shaping the learning preferences of Gen Z, offering diverse and engaging learning experiences that go beyond traditional classrooms.

YouTube has emerged as a dynamic space for educational content, with influencers covering a wide array of subjects ranging from science and mathematics to literature, history, and practical skills. Gen Z, known for its digital savviness, turns to these educational influencers as trusted guides in their quest for knowledge. The appeal lies not only in the accessibility of the platform but also in the interactive and visually engaging nature of the content.

Educational influencers can break down complex concepts into digestible and entertaining formats, making learning more enjoyable and relatable for Gen Z. The informal and conversational style adopted by many of these influencers fosters a sense of connection, creating an environment where learning feels like a conversation with a knowledgeable friend rather than a traditional lecture.

Moreover, the democratization of education through YouTube allows Gen Z to explore niche topics and perspectives that may not be readily available in formal educational settings. Whether it's delving into the intricacies of astrophysics, learning a new language, or acquiring practical life skills, educational influencers provide a wealth of diverse and specialized knowledge that caters to the unique interests and curiosity of this generation.

The influence of educational influencers extends beyond subject matter expertise; it encompasses a broader ethos of lifelong learning and curiosity. Gen Z, characterized by a desire for autonomy and self-directed learning, is drawn to influencers who embody a passion for continuous education and intellectual exploration. The educational content on YouTube has become a dynamic and evolving resource that adapts to the changing needs and interests of Gen Z, fostering a culture of curiosity, self-improvement, and knowledge sharing in the digital age.

The Gen Z Love

Are the new generations giving up on love? What does love look like in the age of convenience and instant communication? Does the prevalent self-medication with alcohol and drugs create an alternative and confusing reality of pleasure and togetherness?

A human body responding to one's highest values as against the trite and banal motions of bedroom sport. Could the series of intimate encounters be causing fragmentation of the self and soul? Emotional reality is granular, even angular. The new-age cacophony of self-love depletes people of empathy and that ability to view and witness the other.

Is perfection in relationships attainable? Does life guarantee an ever-after happiness? Can two people each be more important than the relationship itself? Does life have to be so "together and sorted" before finding a partner, what happened to growing older together? Love is many splendored things; it is also layered and nuanced and complex. But most of all, love is a decision. The decision to commit with a sense of responsibility and accountability. It is important to appreciate the purpose of love, the boundaries involved as well as the shortcomings.

So, what is the research saying about Gen Z? That marriage is desirable but first comes establishing and achieving financial independence. That means freedom of choice in matters of place of work and living. It also means the confidence to express oneself and hold opinions and participate in decision-making with authority. It means being prepared for leadership opportunities. Certainly, love can come later for this generation! Not as late as with the millennials though.

The LinkedIn Parody

Full disclosure! I frowned when my daughter used "informal" language and "inappropriate "emotion" on LinkedIn. LinkedIn, I thought, is a place for thought leaders, not balloon prickers. LinkedIn is a forum of strict decorum, not meant for colourful self-expression.

Woe betides a LinkedIn profile that brags without humility, this is no place for speaking your real truths. Stay out therefore, Gen Z. You may be the largest living generation, the most tech savvy, most at home on social media. Of course, you are educated and hard-working and influential with a credible purchasing power, but you are too funny and authentic and LinkedIn is serious business!

LinkedIn says it hosts millions of open jobs at any given time and any number of professionals are grabbing them, they are conducting business, recruiting talent, generating leads, forming great connections, and teaching and learning. Except for Gen Z! This generation does not enjoy being on LinkedIn. They zoom in to look for jobs and zoom out in the next second without connecting or browsing. LinkedIn overwhelms them and adds to their feelings of insecurity and inadequacy, this research says: https://bixaresearch.com/blog/2020/11/6/Gen Z-linkedin

To get their own back at the platform, Gen Z makes viral parodies of LinkedIn. There are fictitious listings with restaurant names like "The Krusty Krab". This subversive culture inspires TikTok videos, a Twitter handle @LinkedinFlex and a Reddit community that goes by the name LinkedIn Lunatics.

Can LinkedIn afford to fail the young? This is a fearless generation talking. Is anyone listening?

The DIY Content Creation

Generation Z has emerged as a driving force behind the trend of DIY (Do It Yourself) content creation, redefining the landscape of entertainment by showcasing their creativity through homemade music, vlogs, and various other forms of self-produced content. This shift not only challenges traditional entertainment models but also reflects the generation's desire for authentic, relatable, and diverse forms of expression.

At the heart of DIY content creation is the empowerment of individuals to become creators in their own right. Gen Z, armed with accessible technology like smartphones, affordable cameras, and user-friendly editing software, has democratized content production. This generation is leveraging these tools to craft narratives, share experiences, and showcase talents in a way that transcends the polished, high-budget productions of traditional media.

Homemade music has become a powerful avenue for self-expression within Gen Z. Platforms like SoundCloud and YouTube provide aspiring musicians the ability to share their music globally without the need for record labels or elaborate studio setups. DIY musicians can experiment with diverse genres, collaborate with other creators, and build dedicated fan bases, demonstrating that talent and passion are often more crucial than industry connections.

Vlogs, short for video blogs, have also become a staple of Gen Z's content creation. Everyday individuals are transforming their lives into engaging visual narratives, documenting everything from travel adventures to daily routines. This raw and unfiltered approach resonates with audiences who appreciate the authenticity and relatability of these personal stories, challenging the curated perfection often associated with mainstream media.

The trend of DIY content creation fosters a culture of creativity, experimentation, and inclusivity. Gen Z's embrace of diverse voices and perspectives is evident in the vast array of content available online, which goes beyond mainstream narratives. This generation is not just passive consumers of entertainment but active contributors, shaping a digital landscape that reflects their values and interests.

DIY content creation has become a defining characteristic of Gen Z's cultural expression. Through homemade music, vlogs, and other self-produced content, this generation challenges traditional entertainment norms, emphasizing the importance of authenticity, creativity, and the democratization of storytelling in the digital age.

The Self-Critics

There is one challenge the new generations face that we did not. A ruthless, no holds barred comparison with their peers, thank you connectedness.

This scrutiny is brutal. Millennials have to be doing something truly exceptional or important or fulfilling for them to feel they deserve to live; it can get that bad. There are reasons for this seismic self-esteem!

The highly curated and filtered social media posts give a lie to the messiness that is real life. And even though, the young might know this in theory, the glitter of misrepresented posts deflates them, making them feel small. Then there is the omnipresent generic media, with its puffy lists such as the Forbes 30 Under 30. These early successes are rare and the hyped-up stories gloss over factors like luck, timing, connections, and the long trails of unrewarding steps.

Lest we forget, the young are also drowning in self-improvement advice. Adam Philips writes in his book entitled "Missing Out: In Praise of the Unlived life", that "we are always haunted by the myth of our potential." Modern society's record is stuck on realizing one's dreams. These hypothetical futures exist beyond revolving doors that never seem to close.

Perhaps what is needed is one's own inner theme. A very personal golden compass that keeps millennials grounded and directed at the same time. It may also help to remember that the lifespans are longer and there is more time to achieve life and career goals. Some solitude would also help strengthening internal standards of success rather than external expectations.

The Eco-Conscious Influencers

The rise of eco-friendly influencers marks a notable shift in the landscape of digital influence, particularly within Generation Z. In an era characterized by heightened environmental awareness, these influencers wield their online presence to drive sustainable lifestyle choices, promoting ethical consumption and fostering a deeper sense of environmental consciousness.

Eco-conscious influencers within Gen Z are leveraging their platforms to champion sustainable practices across various facets of life. From promoting cruelty-free beauty products to endorsing zero-waste living, these influencers are at the forefront of a movement that prioritizes eco-friendly alternatives. Their content often includes practical tips, product recommendations, and personal anecdotes that resonate with their audience, inspiring them to adopt greener habits.

One of the key strengths of eco-friendly influencers lies in their ability to make sustainability relatable and accessible. By sharing their own journeys towards more eco-conscious living, they demystify sustainable practices and provide tangible steps for their followers to follow suit. This approach resonates particularly well with Gen Z, a generation known for valuing authenticity and transparency in the influencers they choose to follow.

Social media platforms like Instagram, TikTok, and YouTube serve as powerful mediums for these influencers to amplify their message. Engaging visuals, informative captions, and compelling storytelling contribute to the dissemination of eco-friendly ideals to a global audience. The influence of these individuals extends beyond product recommendations; they inspire a mindset shift, encouraging their followers to consider the environmental impact of their choices.

Furthermore, eco-friendly influencers often collaborate with sustainable brands, creating a mutually beneficial ecosystem that reinforces ethical consumerism. By aligning themselves with brands that prioritize environmental responsibility, these influencers amplify the reach of eco-friendly messages and contribute to the growth of the sustainable market.

The surge in eco-friendly influencers within Generation Z underscores a growing commitment to ethical consumption and environmental awareness. Through their online presence, these influencers are catalysing a cultural shift, inspiring their audience to make mindful choices that contribute to a more sustainable and environmentally conscious future.

The Therapy Scene

My generation depended on their mothers, best friends, and the odd cousin for therapy. At the most, there were agony columns in magazines. Unknowingly, we were triangulating, gaslighting, dumping...committing all the psychological sins that modern therapists are charging a fee to wash today.

Apparently. Indians in particular, are new to this. They can't seem to tell the difference between a professional therapist and a family/friend! To begin with, just as we go to the dentist only when the tooth is on its death bed, we call the therapist from the nucleus of a livewire psychotic crisis. Conversation done, anxiety discharged, fee checked out and it is back to normal life.

There is no general consensus yet on the limits of approaching a psychologist or a psychotherapist. In fact, most can't tell the difference between a psychologist, psychotherapist, and a psychiatrist. There is the inability to observe boundaries with the mental health professional. Clients will often expect them to fix their problems when they are the ones who will have to do the heavy lifting. And the less said about the commercials in private practice, the better. Haggling, holding back payments, payment delays or demanding discounts...it is demoralizing and draining.

Friends and family of psychologists ought to observe a different reciprocity with them. Rather than come to depend on the therapists or stalk them on social media, what is recommended is that the client assume responsibility for their lives. And it is hard but imperative not to jump into a therapist's professional intervention with your child or another relative. Finally, the professional deserves the same payment courtesy that are shown the other medical consultants.

The new generations are becoming more aware of their emotional wellbeing and mental health needs. They would do good to remember that the helper in fact, needs their help.

The Digital Gold

The ranks of those at ease with virtual currency is growing and of course, it is the millennials and Gen Z turning the tide. Their vote for the bitcoin as a safe asset against gold is buffeting the Gen Xers and Boomers along.

Questions abound. Is the bitcoin here to stay? How will it affect the dollar's status as the global reserve currency? Is it really just about money laundering? How great is its potential for misuse?

There is another generational difference involved. Gen Xer parents and Boomer grandparents receive as intangible what is to their young, a physical product. In an already volatile air, the instability of bitcoin pricing makes everyone nervous.

Gold, shares and traditional currencies, are units of exchange for physical economies. But cryptocurrency neither has a central bank holding it up nor the earnings from products and services. What it does have is a generational change in thinking. The fact is that millennials are turning their backs on gold. And ideas and beliefs are powerful enough to move mountains and sceptics.

Gen Z is even more plugged in and for them, more than half their world is online. It exists. It is real. It is authentic. And in time, they can reasonably be expected to include bitcoins in their assets and income. Before that, millennials are poised to come into inheritances in a decade or so.

The time, it is moving. What side of the history are you on?

The Digital Detox

In the era of constant connectivity, Generation Z, often referred to as the "digital natives," is paradoxically spearheading the call for digital detox movements. This generation, born and raised in the age of smartphones and social media, recognizes the potential drawbacks of excessive screen time and is actively advocating for a more balanced and mindful approach to technology usage.

The digital detox movement within Gen Z is fuelled by a growing awareness of the impact of prolonged digital engagement on mental health. Recognizing the correlation between excessive screen time, stress, and anxiety, members of this generation are championing the need for periodic breaks from the digital realm. The ubiquity of smartphones and the constant barrage of information have prompted Gen Z to question the effects of this digital saturation on their well-being.

Central to the digital detox movement is the emphasis on fostering offline connections. Gen Z acknowledges the importance of genuine, face-to-face interactions in maintaining mental and emotional health. Social media platforms, while instrumental in connecting individuals across the globe, are seen as potential sources of comparison, competition, and unrealistic standards. In response, members of Gen Z are actively seeking moments of unplugged authenticity, recognizing the value of genuine human connection away from the curated digital spaces.

Additionally, the digital detox movement reflects a desire for a more balanced lifestyle. Gen Z, known for its entrepreneurial spirit and commitment to personal growth, understands the importance of taking breaks to recharge and rejuvenate. Digital detoxes serve as a means to reclaim time for self-reflection, hobbies, and activities that nourish the mind and body.

The digital detox movement within Generation Z signifies a nuanced approach to technology use, emphasizing the importance of mental health, offline connections, and a balanced lifestyle. This advocacy demonstrates a keen awareness of the potential pitfalls of excessive digital immersion and a commitment to cultivating a more mindful and intentional relationship with technology.

The Great Resignation

Word has it that a majority of the workforce around the world is re-evaluating their work choices. It is being spoken of as the impending "Great Resignation". One reason is the ambivalence involved. No one seems sure of what the work week will look like in offices. Will it be a hybrid work model or a full-fledged grand reopening?

The HR fraternity is hard put to gauge precisely what is going on in the minds of their young employees in particular, even as HR leaders revise and reframe policies. The pandemic has certainly caused a loss of connection in companies. Exhaustion and burnout have become pedestrian terms. Then there are the sought after skill-sets that have changed overnight. Many employees have felt forced to join training and skill development programs to prepare for a work change. Some have also tried out new gigs, they have re-discovered their passions and even realigned their professional goals. WFH flexibility has clearly become an expectation with many.

Were companies able to be engaging enough with their remote teams? Who is to say? Did market volatility keep the appraisals way low below the expected mark? Who is to say? One thing is for sure. Everyone in the marketplace got the pandemic gift of time and space to re-boot and re-assess and their conclusions are bound to influence work choices in the coming years.

The strobe light will be trained on factors of work choices, location, flexibility, physical as well as mental wellbeing, data security, compliance, employee engagement, and effective vaccination drives. The workplace dynamics and employee expectations will never be the same again. The old generation workplace has changed for keeps as have the foundations of attrition and retention.

The Virtual Friendships

In the digital age, the notion of friendship has undergone a transformative evolution, with Generation Z at the forefront of forging meaningful connections in the virtual realm. Virtual friendship has become a central aspect of Gen Z's social landscape, extending well beyond the boundaries of physical proximity, and redefining the traditional contours of companionship.

Gaming, social media platforms, and various virtual spaces have emerged as the crucibles for the cultivation of virtual friendships. Online gaming, in particular, serves as a dynamic arena where individuals from diverse backgrounds converge to collaborate, compete, and build lasting bonds. Whether navigating virtual worlds together or strategizing in multiplayer games, Gen Z seamlessly integrates friendship into their digital escapades.

Social media platforms play an instrumental role in expanding the horizons of virtual friendship. Platforms like Instagram, Snapchat, and TikTok provide avenues for expression, communication, and shared experiences. Through curated profiles and real-time updates, Gen Z fosters connections that transcend physical limitations, allowing them to form bonds with like-minded individuals from across the globe.

Virtual spaces, ranging from forums and chat rooms to virtual events, offer Gen Z the opportunity to connect with others who share common interests and passions. These spaces act as virtual meeting grounds, facilitating the exchange of ideas, experiences, and support among individuals who may never meet face-to-face.

The depth of virtual friendships is evident in the emotional investment and support that characterize these relationships. Shared laughter, empathetic conversations, and even digital gestures convey a sense of closeness that challenges the notion that physical proximity is a prerequisite for meaningful connections. Gen Z's virtual friendships often transcend the digital divide, influencing their social dynamics and enriching their lives in ways that were once unimaginable.

In essence, the concept of friendship has transcended physical boundaries in the era of virtual connectivity. Gen Z's adeptness at forming deep relationships through gaming, social media, and virtual spaces reflects a profound shift in the way friendships are forged and sustained, emphasizing the adaptability of human connection in the face of technological evolution.

The Corporate Conscience

Gone are the days when the rare person took a stand. It was considered rude, inconvenient, and too forward. In the new human ocean of social movements like Farmers Movement, Pinjra Tod, Black Lives Matter and MeToo it is the Gen Zers who are fighting the sharks and the jelly fish!

They are able to connect with distant cultures, faraway issues and cutting news faster and earlier and more often than any generation gone before. It keeps them fluid, burning with the fire of social justice and liberally lubricated. Not only are they socially conscious as consumers, they expect the companies they work for to have a corporate conscience. The majority of them hold progressive opinions. A brand's taking a stand on social issues will influence their purchasing decision. They expect big firms to address burning injustices. And lip service alone will not do.

But does that mean a company's social impact initiatives will attract Gen Z talent? Well, a RippleMatch research has it that they are at least as important to them as their compensation packages and the company culture. There seems to be a gender angle too. It is the Gen Z women who are relatively more fired up politically and civically.

It would therefore be tempting to conclude that not only would investment in social impact be the moral high road to take, it would also give a company the competitive edge when recruiting the next generation talent.

The Generational Trauma

If you leave behind a part of you in every place that you inhabited and a bit of that place lives on inside you, what happens if you never lived in a place and yet it breathes within you?

4 Chak, 1L, Tehsil Okara, District Montgomery, Pakistan. I inherited the trauma of my ancestor's violent departure from this home they lived in more than 20 years before my birth. They stamped their stories of horrific train rides, torch bearing marauders and cremation of valuables on my tales. History has an epigenetic effect on our bodies. Our genes are controlled not just by our own experiences but by those of our forefathers. Memories we don't realize we store, express themselves both physically and metaphysically.

It is called generational trauma. The Russians using colourful plastic toy bombs to target children, the rubble of life in Afghanistan, the bullet pockmarks on shaking walls, the wet earth smell of fresh graves, the shutdown of schools, interruption of food supplies, large scale displacement of humans, the assault on homes and families...it will reverberate ahead, across multiple generations as a cortisol fest.

Havens of peace are easy to shatter but they take lifetimes to build. Is peace attainable ever, without war though? Generations will live in the shadow of inherited sorrow. The pall of emigration, war, refugee camps, displacement is a legacy that will hover. The freedom and futures that have been thrown away will haunt generations with guilt, shame and worry.

No matter where an Afghan heart escapes for instance, one chamber will always beat for the homeland.

The Plant Based Lifestyles

The growth of plant-based lifestyles has burgeoned into a prominent cultural shift, with a significant portion of Generation Z adopting plant-based diets as a fundamental aspect of their lives. This trend is propelled by a confluence of factors, including heightened environmental consciousness, a growing awareness of health implications, and a deep-seated commitment to ethical considerations.

Environmental concerns serve as a powerful motivator for many in Gen Z to embrace plant-based living. The industrial livestock sector is a known contributor to greenhouse gas emissions, deforestation, and water pollution. Recognizing the environmental impact of animal agriculture, a generation attuned to climate change and ecological sustainability is increasingly choosing plant-based diets as a means of reducing their carbon footprint. This conscientious choice aligns with the values of environmental stewardship that have become integral to the identity of many in Gen Z.

Parallelly, health considerations play a pivotal role in the adoption of plant-based lifestyles. With an abundance of information readily accessible, Gen Z is well-versed in the potential health benefits associated with plant-based diets. The reduced risk of chronic diseases, lower cholesterol levels, and enhanced overall well-being are compelling factors that drive individuals toward plant-centric nutrition. Social media platforms and online communities amplify the dissemination of health-related information, creating a supportive environment that encourages the pursuit of plant-based living.

Ethical considerations form another cornerstone of the plant-based movement within Gen Z. As advocates for animal welfare, this generation is increasingly concerned about the ethical implications of industrialized animal farming. The shift towards plant-based diets is, for many, a conscious rejection of the practices associated with animal agriculture, driven by a desire to minimize harm to sentient beings.

The growth of plant-based lifestyles within Generation Z represents a multifaceted movement fuelled by environmental consciousness, health awareness, and ethical considerations. As this generation continues to redefine cultural norms, their embrace of plant-based living stands as a testament to a collective commitment to a more sustainable, compassionate, and health-conscious future.

The Real Young

I am a boomer cusper, born at the beginning of Gen X age range. It means I was at the receiving end of millennial lectures on "following life's passion" and "impact of work" and their "to die for Tiramisu"! They also said I had merely made a living while they were actually living! And adulting.

It is nice to have Gen Z take their sails down a bit now. The leaves have turned, and a new generation is at the helm. Look how unfashionably the millennials point their laptop cameras, it is tragic, the propping action they take which gives everyone an unflattering downward angle view of their faces. The Zoomers are saying this, not me.

Also, millennials, the world may have had enough of oversharing. Gen Z is keenly interested in privacy, data security and online honesty. With the surfeit of messaging apps, emails are appearing superfluous to them. And you may no longer be clubbed with Gen Z as an acronym for youth.

Consider your social media brands. As per a prediction by the Oxford Internet Institute, dead people will outnumber the living on Facebook within the next five decades. Insta perfection is already coming off as fake and embarrassing. And parents and grandparents, beware of creating a digital footprint on behalf of your

Gen Z. They know all about how it enriches the big tech companies. Skilled at online activism, they are probably waiting for the millennials to look at themselves in the right camera angle so they know they are fast approaching middle age!

The Remote Socializing

In the ever-evolving landscape of social interaction, the emergence of remote socializing has become a defining characteristic of the Gen Z experience. Virtual hangouts and online gaming have not merely replaced traditional forms of socializing but have redefined the very essence of social connection for this generation.

One of the most striking aspects of this trend is the dissolution of physical boundaries. Gen Z individuals find themselves engaged in conversations and shared experiences with peers from across the globe, transcending geographical limitations that once restricted social circles. Virtual hangouts, facilitated by platforms like Zoom, Microsoft Teams, and various social media applications, have become digital meeting spaces where friends can gather, chat, and engage in activities as if they were in the same room.

Online gaming, in particular, has become a powerful catalyst for global socialization. Games provide a shared virtual environment where individuals can collaborate, compete, and build friendships irrespective of their physical location. Multiplayer games, such as Fortnite, Among Us, and Minecraft, serve as the backdrop for social interactions, fostering a sense of camaraderie that extends beyond the gaming experience itself.

The prevalence of remote socializing has also reshaped the concept of social events. Birthdays, celebrations, and even casual get-togethers are now hosted virtually, allowing Gen Z to maintain connections with friends and family regardless of distance. Virtual events often include creative elements, such as online quizzes, themed backgrounds, and collaborative digital activities, adding a unique flair to the virtual social experience.

Moreover, the integration of technology into socializing has given rise to a new form of expression. Emojis, GIFs, and other digital nuances have become integral to communication, allowing individuals to convey emotions and reactions in ways that transcend traditional text-based conversations.

In essence, remote socializing has become a cornerstone of Gen Z's social landscape, fostering global connections, redefining social events, and integrating technology into the very fabric of social interaction. As this generation continues to navigate the digital realm, the boundaries of traditional social norms are continually expanding, giving rise to a new era of interconnectedness that transcends physical limitations.

The Internet's Successor

Have you checked out the price of Oculus headsets yet? You don't have much choice here; Mark Zuckerberg has unleashed access to the "multiverse" and the workwear will be need to access it.

The Workrooms feature from Facebook's Horizon platform is here, a virtual reality space for most activities deemed human. It is being called the internet's successor. An online world of virtual reality, augmented reality, including the traditional 2D video or audio.

You have workrooms there for meetings including whiteboards with collaborative features. It is technology's response to the current and future virtuality.

We are entering the next big stage of social media. A 3D matrix like internet, straddling the tangible and intangible, complete with equalitarian communities, inexhaustible offices, unending games. Imagine multiverse virtual worlds functioning like new nations without physical borders and complex political and economic systems to engage with the physical reality.

This is bold. How is the state reacting to the Big Tech's mega shifts? There are the five bipartisan antitrust bills. There is the call for industry regulation.

In an interview to the multimedia website VERGE, Zuckerberg says: Facebook is invested heavily in virtual reality "because it's the technology that delivers the clearest form of presence." And that "Flattening out distance creates a lot more opportunities for people."

The CEO said their "infinite office" will let users set up their ideal workplace via a VR headset wherever they are. And that the worldwide shift to working online justifies and heightens the value of metaverse.

I guess we should head to create an account at workrooms.com and invite each other! The collaborative movement is for real.

The Meme Culture Impact

Meme culture, with its witty, often humorous images and captions, has become a pervasive and influential phenomenon that extends far beyond the realms of internet subcultures. Originating as a form of online expression, memes have evolved into a powerful cultural force that shapes conversations, reflects societal trends, and even influences mainstream media.

One of the most significant impacts of meme culture is its ability to spread ideas rapidly and engage a broad audience. Memes leverage humor, relatability, and cultural references to convey messages in a concise and shareable format. This has made them a potent tool for social commentary, allowing individuals to express opinions on a wide range of topics, from politics to pop culture, in a format that is easily digestible and shareable.

Memes also play a crucial role in shaping internet culture and identity. Shared experiences, inside jokes, and references to niche subcultures are encapsulated in memes, creating a sense of community among online users. Memes have the power to define and reinforce group identities, fostering a sense of belonging among those who understand and participate in the meme-sharing culture.

Moreover, meme culture has transcended its digital origins to influence mainstream media and marketing.

Companies and advertisers recognize the power of memes to capture the attention of younger audiences and often incorporate meme formats and humor into their campaigns. This blending of meme culture with mainstream media reflects a broader trend where internet culture increasingly shapes and intersects with the wider cultural landscape.

However, the rapid evolution and turnover of memes also highlight the ephemeral nature of internet culture. What is trendy today may become outdated tomorrow, contributing to a fast-paced and ever-changing digital landscape. Despite this transience, the impact of meme culture endures, leaving an indelible mark on how we communicate, share information, and construct our cultural narratives in the digital age.

The Reverse Ageism

Watch your tone and content when messaging to older people. This is of international importance!

The world is still talking to older people as though they are fragile, alone, and cognitively impaired. But aging has transformed and hopefully the marketers, policy makers and the health sector is paying heed. The new formula for age segmentation is years left in life and not decades since birth. Describing someone "in their 60s" or "in their 80s" cannot be presumed to mean what it was once. There is a wane in dementia which is being credited to higher education and improved cardiovascular health. In fact, given the stress levels millennials and Gen Z deal with, it is the older who seem a lot less isolated and more fulfilled by comparison.

Chronological age is becoming an irrelevant marker more and more. This does not mean however, that the shifting time horizons do not influence messages received. As a matter of fact, it also helps to depict the senior citizens as they see themselves and not as how the younger generations see them.

However, ageism cuts both ways. In cases of "reverse ageism" it is the young professionals at the receiving end of stereotypical age assumptions. Senior leaders may overlook feedback from the junior employees. They may have trouble trusting their younger colleagues with prestigious projects. What if the young are having to deal with far greater racism and sexism than the older workers?

The protection against ageism in some companies and industries needs to apply to young professionals too. That is the only way to accomplish cross generational knowledge transfer and succession planning.

Ageism breeds mistrust.

The Second Generation

The traditional perspective of family businesses involves an entrepreneurial founder followed by a passive second generation, living in his shadow.

The reality could be more complex and, in some cases, better. There are umpteen stories of the unsung heroes in the generation that takes over the family's golden goose. Not only do they uphold the legacy they inherit, but many of them also have a robust family orientation. They absorb and transmit the professional practices of their times. It is on their plate to expand the enterprise and make fresh investments. Should they merely oversee or diversify the legacy business? Would it make sense to create a foundation? How does one handle shared property and investments? Ought the family's advisory team to be retained?

Invariably, it is the family pillar that follows the well-developed enterprise pillar. It is with the second generation that the family shifts from pure business development to broader initiatives. This is the time to cultivate communication and cohesion. It is also at this stage that information sharing, and decision making become more democratic.

With the new generation, the primary focus may be on what to do with the wealth and not how to create more.

This may become their opportunity to be more than mere passive heirs and consumers. The choices they make will decide the family's destiny. The choices of collaborating with, educating and inspiring the family. It is the voices of the younger family members that extol modern perspectives that incorporate social values that the next generation holds dear.

An emotionally intelligent advisory team that also holds a positive view of the next generation can help strike the right balance between the family side of governance and the enterprise side of the family. The second generation can thus be better than the second best.

The Remote Work Revolution

The Remote Work Revolution has emerged as a transformative force, reshaping the landscape of work and challenging traditional notions of office-centric employment. Fuelled by advancements in technology, changing attitudes towards work-life balance, and the global response to the COVID-19 pandemic, remote work has become a mainstream phenomenon, offering unprecedented flexibility and opportunities for both employers and employees.

One of the key drivers of this revolution is the advent of sophisticated communication and collaboration tools. Video conferencing, project management software, and instant messaging platforms have enabled seamless connectivity across time zones, fostering collaboration among teams spread across the globe. This technological infrastructure has not only made remote work feasible but has also demonstrated that productivity and innovation can thrive outside the confines of a physical office.

The pandemic acted as a catalyst, accelerating the adoption of remote work practices. As organizations implemented remote work policies to ensure business continuity, they discovered the benefits of a decentralized workforce. Reduced overhead costs, improved employee satisfaction, and access to a global talent pool are among the advantages that have prompted many companies to embrace remote work as a long-term strategy.

Employees, too, have experienced a shift in expectations. The desire for a better work-life balance, reduced commute times, and the ability to customize their work environment have led many to prefer remote work arrangements. This shift in employee preferences has forced companies to rethink their traditional office-centric models and consider hybrid or fully remote setups to attract and retain top talent.

However, the Remote Work Revolution also presents challenges. Organizations must navigate issues related to maintaining company culture, ensuring effective communication, and addressing potential feelings of isolation among remote workers. Striking the right balance between flexibility and structure is crucial for the sustained success of remote work initiatives.

The Remote Work Revolution signifies a paradigm shift in the way we approach work. As technology continues to evolve and the benefits of remote work become more apparent, it is likely that this revolution will continue to shape the future of work, influencing how and where people collaborate to drive innovation and business success.

The Non-Saaya Days

'*Saaya'* days are the auspicious Hindu marriage dates in my corner of the world. But COVID-19 has transformed the new-generation weddings.

Gone are the big fat Indian marriages. Non-saaya dates are the new operational. The superstitions around restricted dates and seasons are out of the window. A list of non-saaya dates in fact, is doing the rounds, getting snapped up at a roar!

The traditional, astrology inclined Indian mindset has shifted gears admirably to accommodate the new limitations. The guest lists are slimmer, the venues deliberately kept within easy reach, no risking unforeseen govt. regulations. An intimate, stress free and peaceful affair is the current event goal.

With just four months left of the year 2021, there are only a handful of *saaya* dates available. For some couples, there have already been postponements and patience may be running thin. So even though, the earlier generations did not wed between July to November because the supreme power was believed to be resting during that time, the young are not left much choice. And for once, tradition has shown agility by quickly calculating "*shubh mahurat*" even on non-saaya days using the couple's natal charts.

Any fears of the Covid return in November are similarly being dealt with, using astrological remedies.

Bravo to the millennials for finding the silver lining in personalized evaluations of zodiac signs. With non-*saaya* dates, they are also getting better rates!

The lesson learnt from COVID-19? *Har Din Shubh Hai*! If you are alive, THAT is auspicious.

The White Knights

Everybody is a coach. Everybody wants to help. Everybody wants to transform.

None of this had a chance when I was growing up. We hated asking for help! It was a sign of weakness, an admission of failure, a dumping of disease.

It has never been easier to confess limitations and be honoured for simply wanting to learn. But what if I do not want to enter THE ADVICE TRAP, a book by the author Michael Bungay Stanier. What if I have questions for the Coach, Consultant and Advisor?

1. Do you believe you are better than me?
2. Are you addicted to saving me?
3. Do you see that you are helping yourself by helping me?
4. Will it make you happy seeing me succeed without your help?

Psychology has a name for this. It is called the "White Knight Syndrome". An addiction to being an "agency" to another. May be the new-generation shift in company cultures ought to consider both sides of this "vulnerability routine". Perhaps we need a cockpit checklist for the helper!

Pledge, dear Coach to let your coachees suffer the consequences of their poor choices.

Pledge, dear Consultant to bring your clients to a point of not needing you anymore.

Pledge, dear Leader to deliver unvarnished truth, no matter how painful, in a respectful manner.

To help another is a prerogative. The best way perhaps is to begin by doing no harm. And that may mean differentiating what we are from what we do. Helping could be giving and not merely being!

The New Generation Dysmorphia

New generation dysmorphia refers to the modern phenomenon where individuals, particularly the younger generation, experience a heightened sense of dissatisfaction or distress related to their appearance, fueled by the pervasive influence of social media, unrealistic beauty standards, and the constant comparison with others. This emerging trend is a distinct manifestation of body dysmorphic tendencies influenced by the digital age.

In the era of Instagram, Snapchat, and other image-centric platforms, the portrayal of idealized beauty has reached unprecedented levels. Filters, photo-editing apps, and curated feeds contribute to a distorted perception of reality, leading individuals to perceive their own appearance through an unrealistic lens. The incessant exposure to carefully crafted images of flawless faces and bodies can contribute to feelings of inadequacy, fostering a sense of new generation dysmorphia.

Moreover, the pressure to conform to societal beauty standards and gain approval through online validation can intensify these dysmorphic tendencies. The constant comparison with digitally altered images of influencers and celebrities can erode self-esteem, leading to an unhealthy preoccupation with one's physical appearance. The pursuit of an unattainable ideal can contribute to mental health challenges, including anxiety, depression, and body dysmorphic disorder.

New generation dysmorphia is also associated with the phenomenon of "Snapchat dysmorphia," where individuals seek cosmetic procedures to resemble their filtered or digitally enhanced selves. The desire to match the flawless images presented on social media platforms can drive a dangerous pursuit of perfection, often fuelled by the fear of falling short of the digitally manipulated standards of beauty.

Addressing new generation dysmorphia requires a multi-faceted approach. It involves fostering digital literacy, promoting body positivity, and encouraging a more authentic representation of oneself on social media. Additionally, mental health support and education on the potential pitfalls of excessive digital comparison can play a crucial role in mitigating the impact of new generation dysmorphia. Ultimately, creating a culture that values diversity, authenticity, and self-acceptance is essential for combating the adverse effects of distorted beauty standards in the digital age.

The Right to Repair

Who knew the government would have to pass a legislation to give back to the citizens the right to repair their lamps, dishwashers, vacuum cleaners, computer, smartphones, and TV receivers? The older generations took this so much for granted. My family still owns my grandparents' vintage Gramaphone.

Along came the waste-based economy. Manufacturers began creating products made of soldered and glued parts that are so riveted, it is impossible to open them. The idea of provisions to upgrade and adapt devices to match up to new technical standards had no buyers.

That may be changing with the new generation anti-waste law with a repair index. The factors used to calculate this score will include ease of disassembly, access to repair information, and price and availability of spare parts. France in particular is targeting 60 percent of electronic equipment to be repairable by 2026. The energy-efficiency based eco-design regulations will henceforth define standards for repair and useful life.

E-waste streams are overflowing in Europe. The move to regulate harmful consumer waste finds favour with nearly 80 percent of EU citizens who would rather repair than replace. There is a growing demand in fact, to have manufacturers be obliged to facilitate a sustainable circular economy.

These new eco-design guidelines and right to repair mandates coming from one of the world's largest markets is sure to resound in all parts of the world. And the biggies are listening. Apple has launched a repair program for individual businesses. Companies have access to Apple parts, tools, and training to perform out-of-warranty repairs.

Two things will be crucial to this goal of climate-neutrality. Will the policy makers stand up to the manufacturers' lobbies? Will mindsets alter in tandem with the gadgets being fixed?

The Succession Sketches

Times were when knowledge transfer and succession planning were directed at senior leaders on the verge of retirement. But the new generations are not staying long enough. The exit door is revolving like never before, the entire generational spectrum swinging through.

Who is calculating the associated leakages of intellectual capital? An exit interview may be too late for any meaningful recovery of documents related to best practices, key performance indicators or even half-drafted initiatives. Only an ongoing documentation protocol will ensure protection against unexpected departures and the challenge of building new leaders.

Agile new generations rise fast, act faster and quit fastest! The management ideas they implement, the critical business intelligence they gather, the creative workflows that take shape can only be compiled through a cross-generational strategy. The pro-active habit of reflecting upon and filing regularly all the research findings, job descriptions, event guidelines, product playbooks is a collaborative contribution to future success of the company that needs to be consciously cultivated.

The older generations held their cards close to the heart, there was the inner circle and tricks of the trade shared with the chosen few. That is too big a risk today.

Teams have to build the ability to bounce back from scratch in record time from worst case scenarios.

Succession sketches need to be ready. Your crucial tasks. Your frequent problems. Your solutions that worked. And in an ideal situation, visualize yourself handing it over while negotiating the revolving door!

This would be the mission of intergenerational management.

The Sologamy

Sologamy, a term derived from "solo" and "monogamy," is a contemporary phenomenon where individuals choose to marry themselves. While unconventional, sologamy has gained attention as a symbolic and empowering expression of self-love and independence. This trend reflects evolving attitudes toward relationships, marriage, and the pursuit of personal happiness.

In a sologamous ceremony, individuals make vows to themselves, committing to self-acceptance, self-improvement, and a lifelong partnership with their own well-being. The act is not legally binding in the traditional sense, as there is no legal recognition of marrying oneself, but it serves as a personal and symbolic declaration of self-love.

Advocates of sologamy argue that it offers a unique opportunity for self-reflection and personal growth. In a world where societal expectations and norms often place emphasis on finding a life partner, sologamy encourages individuals to prioritize their own happiness and well-being. It challenges the notion that one's worth is tied to external relationships and emphasizes the importance of cultivating a positive relationship with oneself.

Critics, on the other hand, may view sologamy as a rejection of traditional values or an unnecessary departure from conventional relationship structures. However, proponents argue that it is not a rejection of partnerships but rather an affirmation of individuality and self-respect.

Sologamy has gained visibility through public ceremonies and social media, where individuals share their experiences and reasons for choosing this path. Some see it as a response to the increasing emphasis on self-care and mental health, encouraging people to prioritize their own needs and happiness before seeking validation or fulfilment through external relationships.

While sologamy may not be for everyone, its emergence as a social phenomenon signals a broader shift in societal attitudes toward self-love and independence. It challenges conventional expectations around marriage and relationships, encouraging individuals to celebrate and commit to their own personal journey of growth and fulfilment. Sologamy, in essence, is a declaration that one's happiness and completeness can be found within oneself.

The Age Polarities

I have been told, "Why don't you sit back and relax now? Hand it over!"

Lie still you mean? Atrophy? Go into a slow decline? Play five hours of golf to justify my existence? Go on a touristy EU tour so as to validate the script of, "You are permitted to have some fun now!"

It all sounds like an exercise in dressing up the wait to die. And that is fine if YOU want it that way. I am a shade more eager to expand. And ambition is not always about fame and money; it is about the challenge of living with a shimmer and flair. It is about creating. It is about straining all the faculties one is fortunate to own.

Looks, brands, marquee banners are not half as attractive as the human mind and spirit, stretching towards a vision. The stubborn stamina to go on and on. That is the real-life fuel.

Both the consumers and the markets are aging. The marketer's favourite age bracket of 18 to 34 is no longer watertight. There is a new cross-generational wave cresting to which the older lot bring stamina, discipline and commitment that can more than match the ideas and passion and fearless direction of the young. Just as binaries are dissolving elsewhere, the polarities of age are ebbing.

Age may not therefore be a factor alone in recruitment for great jobs.

Seeding age diversity could well be the strategic solution to the problems of the day after tomorrow. I believe that success in every shape and size today will depend more and more on harnessing generational diversity.

The Generational Values

Generational differences in values reflect the evolving cultural landscape and societal shifts that occur over time. Each generation, shaped by its unique historical, technological, and economic context, develops distinct perspectives, priorities, and ethical frameworks. Understanding these variations in values is essential for fostering effective communication and cooperation across different age groups.

Traditionalists, born before 1946, often value hard work, loyalty, and respect for authority. Shaped by the aftermath of World War II and the Great Depression, they tend to emphasize stability, discipline, and a strong work ethic. Baby Boomers, born between 1946 and 1964, share a commitment to social change and individual expression. They value prosperity, achievement, and often prioritize job security.

Generation X, born between 1965 and 1980, witnessed the advent of technology and the rise of dual-career families. Independence, adaptability, and skepticism characterize their values. Millennials, born between 1981 and 1996, grew up amid rapid technological advancements and globalization. They often prioritize work-life balance, inclusivity, and social responsibility.

Generation Z, born from the mid-1990s to the early 2010s, is marked by digital nativism, inclusivity, and a penchant for activism. They value authenticity, diversity, and environmental sustainability. These values are shaped by a world where information is instantaneously accessible, and social justice issues are at the forefront of public discourse.

Understanding these generational differences in values is crucial for businesses, educational institutions, and communities aiming to create inclusive environments. It helps bridge communication gaps, promotes collaboration, and encourages the exchange of ideas. Recognizing the strengths each generation brings to the table fosters a more dynamic and innovative society, where diverse values coexist and contribute to a richer, more comprehensive understanding of the world. Embracing these differences allows for the cultivation of a collective wisdom that transcends generational boundaries, fostering a society that learns from the past while adapting to the ever-changing present and future.

The Inorganic Formula

Back in our days, to become a cyclist, you had to climb up, fall often, dust off the pain and keep at it. It was clear as day that there was no way to become a writer without writing. To swim, you had to splutter and sink and be thumped on the back and deal with the ball of fear gurgling in your limbs.

It seems now that the rules have changed. You can learn to be a 'thought leader' without ever spouting one original idea. No training on thought leadership breathes a word about 'thinking' which incidentally is the core skill involved.

Becoming an Amazon best-seller is not related directly to a stunning way with words or evocative imagery or a throat catching storyline. It is related to algorithms, smart categorization of one's book and micro marketing.

TEDx and Josh Talks, the speaker's current hallmarks have everyone scrambling for the formula.

You get the drift? The calculation is working backwards. We are not building, we are deconstructing.

A bit ironic, wouldn't you say? After all, human glory and winning ideas have often come from happenstance.

Then there is the associated self-promotion, the hustling for professional status. It used to start outside in; the world conferring superstardom on thinkers like Vijay Govindarajan and Amartya Sen and Ram Charan. But the coaches will have you declare yourself an expertise, a self-proclaimed authority, a world-class professional.

Isn't this formulaic aspiration and projection a bit inorganic?

The Inherited Pain

Inherited pain, an intangible legacy passed down through generations, is a profound aspect of the human experience that transcends time and familial boundaries. It encapsulates the emotional, psychological, and sometimes even physical scars imprinted on individuals by the traumas endured by their ancestors. This silent transmission of suffering can shape the very core of one's identity, influencing behavior, perceptions, and coping mechanisms.

The origins of inherited pain are diverse, ranging from historical atrocities like wars and genocide to personal struggles such as poverty, abuse, or loss. Families unwittingly carry the weight of these experiences, and the repercussions ripple through the descendants, leaving an indelible mark on their psyche. The ghosts of past hardships haunt the present, creating a complex tapestry of emotions that individuals grapple with, often without a clear understanding of their origin.

Navigating inherited pain requires a delicate balance between acknowledging the past and forging a path toward healing. Awareness of the sources of pain can empower individuals to break free from destructive patterns and foster resilience. However, confronting the ghosts of the past is no easy task, as the tendrils of inherited pain may be deeply embedded in family dynamics and cultural narratives.

Therapeutic interventions, both individual and collective, play a crucial role in unravelling inherited pain. By providing a safe space for exploration and expression, therapy becomes a transformative tool in the journey toward understanding, acceptance, and ultimately, healing. Additionally, fostering open conversations within families and communities creates an environment where the burden of inherited pain can be shared and, collectively, lightened.

Inherited pain is a poignant reminder of the interconnectedness of human experiences across time. Acknowledging and addressing this legacy is a courageous step toward breaking the cycle of suffering, offering the possibility of a more liberated and emotionally resilient future for generations to come.

The Fairy Comments

Gen Z (born 1997 – 2012) is killing with kindness on social media through their 'fairy comments'.

Social media gives them the agency and autonomy to unleash their wrath at social injustice. The climate is woke, there is a greater sensitivity to perceived wrongs and tolerance levels are at an all-time low.

So, what are fairy comments? These are one liners, dripping with sarcasm. However, they start off innocently enough but end with an unexpectedly savage twist.

TikTok is the minefield. Consider this example: "Just keep smiling, I love the color yellow!" or "The sky is the limit, stay on the ground." And "God made everyone beautiful, who made you?"

These comments are peppered with fairy-like emojis such as sparklers, rainbows, heart and butterflies and stars. They act as a visual red herring, giving off a misleading heart-warming and positive vibe. They also allow our youngest to vent their sense of impending doom.

Dear adults therefore, do they tickle your dark side? Just for laughs? Would you want to join the fun without taxing your overstimulated brain? Well, there are a host of fairy comment generators on the internet. Give them a try.

Greta Thunberg. Nadya Teresa Okamoto. Zulaikha Patel. The Gen Z leaders are coming together from all corners of the earth to hold companies and leaders and civil society accountable.

And wondrously enough, Indian teens are testing the waters too, despite their wary and survival mode families, schools and culture. For the longest time, youth has been the excluded majority.

Our chickens are coming home to roost!

The Deinfluencer

The authenticity virus has hit our Insta and TikTok influencers! In a complete about turn, they are working overtime urging people not to buy things.

They are saying surprising things. You don't need that lip polishing oil! You don't need that pricey bond-building shampoo! You don't need that micro-sculpting cream!

Lo and behold, the Deinfluencers are the new Influencers. What is going on? Is it because consumers are fatigued with the constant hammering from marketers? Is it that the world's economy is tricky and people are tightening their belts? Maybe, there is a push from our young towards a conscious consumerism.

The signs have been there for a while. Slow fashion, cancelling unscrupulous brands, minimalism, decluttering, coming clean on climate bills...the market needs and wants have been changing. There have been some wider conversations about influencing, spending culture, and TikTok's role in it all, think of the hashtag tiktokmademebuyit.

So, will the honest product critiques stay? The phenomenon of deinfluencing is already adapting to become about "buy this not that". It is perhaps almost impossible to free a platform like TikTok of consumerism.

But the deinfluencers have certainly rocked the boat! They got more following because negative information is more believable. They were able to create a space for people to give their true opinions. For a while now, the deinfluencers' influence has been going up and the influencers influence has been going down.

It remains to be soon who will have a bigger impact on the marketplace. The rising deinfluencers or the declining influencers?

The Curated Existence

It is fascinating how the "curated generation" creates its reality, carefully filtering and editing to present an idealized version. And it is not just Gen Z that is navigating the complexities of self-expression, identity construction, and social validation. This dance straddles a multigenerational horde, hungry for validation and connection. Every move is a potential addition to a considered and crafted narrative.

And it is not about individual Instagram visuals or TikTok's brief videos alone, there are personal brands under construction on social media platforms. One can create an online persona . Young individuals become architects of their own online personas, carefully selecting content that aligns with their desired image. This intentional self-presentation often blurs the lines between the real and the curated, creating a parallel existence where the online self becomes a reflection, if not a projection, of the offline identity.

However, this curated existence is not just about showcasing the highlights. Vulnerability finds its place amidst the curated perfection, as individuals share carefully framed moments of authenticity. The juxtaposition of curated content with genuine moments creates a nuanced tapestry of identity that reflects the multidimensionality of the young experience.

The curated existence also extends to lifestyle choices, with young people seeking out experiences that align with their online personas. From travel destinations to fashion choices, each decision becomes an opportunity to contribute to the overarching narrative of a well-curated life.

Yet, the pursuit of a curated existence brings with it challenges, as the pressure to maintain a flawless facade can lead to anxiety and self-doubt. The curated generation must navigate the delicate balance between authenticity and the desire for social validation, recognizing the importance of genuine connections amidst the curated content that dominates their digital landscapes. In a world where the lines between the curated and the authentic blur, the young find themselves navigating the complexities of self-expression in an ever-evolving digital landscape.

The Aces

Our society is so hyper-sexualized, it is hard for most to comprehend the young and fast-growing asexuality movement. These are the Aces, they do not feel sexual attraction towards others. And no, they are not insecure people or gay or psychopaths who lack the ability to relate and connect with others.

Asexuality has been called the "forgotten" or "invisible" orientation given its lack of public presence. In fact, until late, US's Diagnostic and Statistical Manual of Mental Disorders considered it a medical issue, a form of desire disorder! It has also been referred to as "the world's first internet orientation," implying that the aces were born with the worldwide web.

Well, they are certainly a growing tribe on the internet. A spirited collective of younger activists who give talks, write books, host podcasts, and run YouTube channels. The gen-next is showing it's possible to live a fulfilling life without sex and that there are other paths to human connection.

Yasmin Benoit, the young fashion model, and the world's most prominent asexuality activist, is determined to ensure other asexual people don't feel broken or alone in a worldwide culture of carnality. Aces are optimistic that in time, dating and sex will no longer be viewed as the most legitimate paths to intimacy. It would be entirely feasible to raise a child for instance with your best friend, whether or not you are asexual.

Fancy the impact on humankind! This could allay our deep-seated fear of being alone. By showing that a life filled with close friendships can be meaningful and satisfying – and *enough* – aces seem set to open our minds and lead the way.

The Memes

Who hasn't chuckled at a meme?

Meme is short for mimeme, a Greek word meaning "imitated thing". It is today, one of the fastest ways a culture catches fire.

Memes cause laughs. Memes can create fear. Memes can also misinform. They have been compared by the Utah State University computer science professor Nicholas S. Flann to a "biological virus that infects a host's mind and replicates via the share button." Memes are not just fun, therefore. They influence mass behaviour which then affects the future. Think the 2016 election in the USA and the Arab Spring revolutions in the early 2010s.

We continue to wade through an ecosystem of misinformation online. There is no international code on information integrity as yet. But since the stories we share matter, how do we decide which ones to forward and which to kill?

Dr. Jeannie Banks Thomas, a folklorist and a Fellow of the American Folklore Society has developed the SLAP test to help. SLAP stands for Scare, Logistics, A-list, and Prejudice.

When faced with a new piece of information, ask yourself:

Does it cause a reaction of fear or shock?

Does it rely on a far-fetched set of logistics to be true?

Does the narrative involve A-List celebrities or high-profile companies or events? For instance, is Bill Gates involved?

Does the account play into your own confirmation biases or prejudices? Does it demonize some person or group as a bad actor?

If you answer yes to one of these questions, don't trust the story right off, at the least, explore it. Learn to be suspicious!

The Inclusive Fashion

Gen Z's embrace of inclusive fashion stands out as a powerful and transformative trend, reshaping the industry by championing diversity, representation, and breaking away from traditional beauty norms. This generation is remarkably supportive of fashion that goes beyond stereotypes, celebrating individuality, body positivity, and various expressions of identity.

Inclusive fashion for Gen Z is not merely a trend but a fundamental shift in the perception of beauty. The movement towards inclusivity is evident in the demand for diverse models, sizes, ethnicities, and gender identities on fashion runways, in advertising, and across social media platforms. Gen Z actively seeks out brands and influencers that prioritize representation, creating a positive feedback loop that encourages the industry to be more inclusive.

Social media plays a pivotal role in this phenomenon, serving as a platform for voices that were traditionally marginalized. Gen Z leverages hashtags and viral challenges to promote inclusive fashion, fostering a sense of community where individuals from different backgrounds can share their unique styles and perspectives. This democratization of fashion allows for a more authentic representation of the diverse identities within Gen Z.

Moreover, this generation is quick to call out brands that fail to embrace inclusivity genuinely. Gen Z demands authenticity and transparency, pushing for not just a diverse cast but also diverse leadership and ethical practices within fashion companies. This activism extends beyond online spaces, with Gen Z participating in protests, advocating for fair labor practices, and contributing to a broader conversation about the impact of the fashion industry on the environment.

In essence, Gen Z's support for inclusive fashion is a reflection of their commitment to equality and individuality. By redefining beauty standards and challenging the conventional norms of the fashion industry, this generation is influencing a more accepting and diverse future where everyone feels seen and celebrated in the world of fashion.

Loving Better

Gen Z will be our first generation to run out of emotional cello tape...they break hearts, band aid them and offer them to the next person of interest at a frightening rate. Born after the 1997, technology and mobility has made it easy for them to both make up and break up. How do they cope with this serial renting of their hearts? What price do they and their families pay for this emotional roulette?

It used to be that special friends were replaced before they left. For Gen Z, they just stop talking, block each other on social media and disappear. The lack of closure is deadly. While the millennials struggled with their 'why', Gen Z is thrashing around with their relationships.

They seem to practice the art of letting go in different ways. Find someone new and move on quickly. Depend on support from friends, online communities for validation and digital platforms for self-expression. In some cases, use weed or isolation or new hobbies. Cutting off their hair, pain filled introspection, extreme detachment and putting up personal walls...it can be uphill.

Why should someone walking out mean the end of the world to a young person? It is the way friendship is done today. Best friends know everything about each other and walk away with irreplaceable life chunks when they do, leaving gaping voids behind. Building it all with just one person inevitably leads to anger, pain and sleepless nights.

These life bridges do not need to be broken. They can be lifted. Caringly, compassionately and with a respectful closure.

What does a conversation of self-preservation look like? Is there any wonder there is this new vocabulary around mental health, micro-aggressions and narcissistic abuse? It is worse for those growing up as trans*queer individuals, they live with social boycott and alienation, preparing themselves subconsciously for the possibility of loss.

The science of loving better has a place today. The art of drawing a line could be a life-saving skill for Gen Z. They will need support to stop blocking the door and show people the way out when need be.

The Queer Legacy

It was the 6 Sep 2018. My 26-year-old activist daughter and I were turning around the India Gate on our way to meet her Kathak Guruji. There was a ping on her phone and what followed nearly crashed us on the kerb.

In a landmark judgement, the Indian Supreme Court had decriminalized gay sex/consensual adult sex. And she couldn't hold back her exultation! The arguments were rooted in fundamental rights. In an acknowledgement of our constitution as a living organic document, open to interpretation that nullified inequality and injustice. In the need to give all classes the promise of humanity.

With the removal of Section 377 that day, the LGBTQ community became equal citizens of the nation. Things have gone equivocal since but the disconnect between social morality now and the celebration of queer love in Indian history and mythology has always nagged.

The Section 377 that is often spoken of as a colonial legacy, erased India's rich regional heritage of cultural and religious depictions of homosexual relations. Queer characters in Indian mythology were, in fact, acknowledged as crucial to the narratives, they took the story forward and were celebrated. There was no societal homophobia in the faith systems of the subcontinent nor were there ancient injunctions against transgenders, known as Hijras.

Hinduism clearly acknowledges a third gender and queer sexualities. Asia's first Genderqueer Pride Parade was held in Madurai, Tamil Nadu in 2012. And admirably enough, many intrepid citizens of our country continue to negotiate their democratic rights with the state. The world's largest democracy and a global power on the rise, owes her dynamism to them.

It remains for the law to make pronouncements that can then be used as tools for society to change. Public parks, Hijra-Farsi and Conversion therapies preclude unity in diversity.

The MCS Syndrome

Do you live your life as though it were a music video with you at the centre as its mini rock star? You are not Gen Z, are you?

Is Main character syndrome (MCS) a pop culture phenomenon, an empowering coping mechanism or grist for the therapist's mill?

Fancy walking down a busy road. You are listening to a crime podcast at 2x speed, and two cars crash 100 metres ahead of you. There is mayhem on the highway, but you are now a victim of Post Traumatic Stress Disorder. You click a selfie and upload it on social media with the title, "I am not overreacting. This is the reason for my sadness." You are at that moment living through the "trauma survivor trope".

Yes, it is unreal. Yes, it is self-deprecating. But there is defence for this brand of a personal narrative. One school of thought points out how this may help find meaning and logic in life's experiences. It is healthy and helpful some say, to escape from the periodical hellscapes of regular life. But what if our accident witness fancied himself as a Mafia lord who ordered a deliberate car accident to wipe out a whistleblower?

Although MCS does not have a formal diagnosis, it shares some aspects with narcissism. With MCS, other people are not the Main Character's problem but self-care is. The "main-character-energy" has come to be a much-loved trend with tips on how to create your-own-reality. It may sound empowering on the surface but there is spiritual brittleness in viewing life through a binary lens of heroic victim and evil perpetrator. My generation grew up believing that life was meant to be boring, and that love was an active noun like struggle, not a passive form of self-love.

What are you going to do when your technology and media enabled Gen Z comes in expecting to be placed as Player One? Many of them are not looking at employers for financial security. They see themselves as a resource too.

They might actually want to be the main character. Are you ready?

The Indian *Gen* Z

Not only are India's Gen Z slightly distinct from the global template, but they also differ from each other, depending on their hometowns and social strata.

Born between 1997 and 2012, the global cohort is so diverse, they can't recognize diversity! They entered the world in an era of shifting political power, just as mankind was hitting peak humanity and singularity was preparing to land. Their pen pictures? Hyper progressive viewpoints, gender-fluid expression and a morose mood, the soundtrack to this complicated world being Billi Eilish.

But does this Gen Z portrait apply to India too where collectivist values jostle with globally valued individuality? It largely does among the urban, educated, upper middle-class Indians who live in metropolitan cities, with their liberal upbringing and western exposure. But the Gen Z in tier-two and tier-three cities of India are different. To appreciate this distinction, it is important to first understand what binds them all.

Gen Z everywhere exhibits vertical defiance and horizontal conformity! While they reject parental and societal values of gender expression, caste-based discrimination, and mindless consumption, they discover their clans in peers with online representations. They retain however a puzzling but poignant hesitancy and uncertainty. It has to be the crisis of choice they face, almost a decision paralysis. Be it education, career, gender, life partner, sexual expression...there is confusion galore! What sets Gen Z of India's hinterland apart from their mainland members is the manner in which they respond to this seeming stalemate.

Unlike the Gen Z in the developed world with their powerful sense of one's personal agency, Gen Z in India's second- and third-tier cities still hold onto their rooted cultural values. These serve as anchors as they negotiate the creation of their self-hood in our ambivalent times. The basis for their choices and behaviours is not just their own pleasure or fulfilment but also the social context around them involving parental relationships and societal expectations. And yet, even though they appear to choose the traditional low-risk careers such as engineering or medicine or an MBA, they seem to practice self-determination through their hobbies and interests.

It is not uncommon to find Gen Z in India wearing Zara and Adidas while performing traditional rituals at festivals or rising early for online yoga after pub crawling the night before. This is the brave new world of transculturality and patchwork identities!

The Whistleblower

Nothing separates the new generations from the old as much as their stunning sense of personal agency. The young express themselves, follow their dreams and call out injustices without fear of censure.

Workplaces used to be very different once, essentially pro-establishment. Parents and grandparents were brought up to fit in rather than stand out. They spent their entire lives working at one company, playing by the rules, and climbing the ladder, a step at a time. Little wonder that their office people became an extension of the family. Gratitude was the expected norm as was loyalty for the resources and status their jobs brought them. Looking back, it is hard to imagine them blowing the whistle on their benefactors.

By contrast the modern gig economy presents as a carousel. The entrepreneurs barely stay in one spot long enough to gather any moss. They dart in search of skills, scale, and selfhood. Having discovered their uniqueness and voices, the young also act from an acute sense of social responsibility. They point out the wrongdoings in their environment for the sake of the "larger good".

In India, it was the Right to Information Act 2005 that gave her citizens a potent tool to demand transparency and accountability from any public authority. Numerous

Public Interest Litigations have been used to expose the gaps between promise and delivery. Corporate India has the Companies Act, 2013, that mandated the need to set up vigil mechanisms among listed and specific classes of companies to report corporate malpractice, fraud, misconduct, and non-compliance.

The whistleblower landscape, however, is littered with casualties and confusion. Are whistleblowers heroes or traitors? On whom does the responsibility for ethical behaviour rests? The individual or the collective? Has the generational increase in whistleblowing brought in a matching expansion in whistle-blower protections? Who ensures that the allegations are well-founded and not being misused to settle scores? While the young come into the workforce emboldened by courageous movements, are there policies in place to protect the innocent victims who receive no help to restore their ruined reputations?

The Boundaries

There is a lot of talk on establishing and communicating boundaries in modern therapy. But what are these boundaries? And are they continental in nature?!

Take the Indian subcontinent. People live in extended familial clans here. There are families by birth and then by marriage. Not just parents, there are the grandparents, in-laws, great uncles, and aunts, first and second cousins, siblings, children.

Societies north of equator are highly relational. While the support systems are strong, they also demand adjustment, flexibility, and accommodation. Your very safety net will spout opinions and judgements! Social capital equals social validation like nowhere else in the world perhaps.

How then do you explain to your kith and kin that boundary is a limit you are defining to ensure your welfare by keeping them out? So that they don't joke at your expense. So that you don't get yelled at. So that your partner does not join you at the hip.

It is tricky. Is honouring someone's wish not to share their anguish equivalent to being indifferent to them? In respecting someone's privacy, could you be alienating them from the help they need? Would giving others space to make their mistakes absolve you of the responsibility of sharing the consequences?

First, can I flit about telling the world how to behave with me, specifying what words may or may not be used in my presence? Will these warnings get me what I want? Particularly with Indian friends and family who are born boundary blind!

Boundary setting however, has come to be considered central to being your true self: unique, adequate, and enough. So, what are you going to do? There are bound to be reactions to your drawing the lines. There may be plain reluctance to accept this as a new form of care. You may experience a sense of alienation from your tight but safe inner circle. "One tight slap" parenting has been around so long, the idea of family members individuating will need a caesarean section to come into this world.

The way to set one's boundaries under these circumstances would be to acquire a keen self-awareness first on the why and how of the boundary. Step two would be to communicate gently, in a non-violent way, what you need from those around you. There are no guarantees, and you may end up losing precious people along the way. But given the maze around us, can you risk losing yourself?

In life, there is always a trade off!

The Space Tourism

One of the most intriguing aspects of Gen Z's relationship with space tourism is the fusion of youthful enthusiasm, technological prowess, and a futuristic mindset. Unlike previous generations, Gen Z has grown up in a digital age characterized by rapid technological advancements, and their connection with space tourism reflects this intersection of innovation and aspiration.

Gen Z's interest in space tourism is not merely a fascination with the cosmos but a reflection of their broader outlook on life. The concept of exploring outer space aligns seamlessly with their futuristic mindset, driven by a desire for novel experiences and a belief in the limitless possibilities of technology. Growing up with sci-fi influences and witnessing the privatization of space exploration by companies like SpaceX, Blue Origin, and others, Gen Z envisions a future where space travel is not just for astronauts but accessible to the general public.

This generation's engagement with space tourism extends beyond passive interest; it embodies a proactive approach. Gen Z is not content with being mere spectators; they are keenly involved in discussions about the ethical considerations, environmental impact, and the potential societal implications of space tourism. Their conversations extend to issues like responsible space tourism practices, sustainable space exploration, and the importance of preserving celestial environments.

Moreover, Gen Z utilizes social media platforms and online communities to share and shape their views on space tourism. Influencers and content creators within this generation leverage their platforms to discuss the possibilities and challenges of space travel, creating a dynamic dialogue that reaches a global audience.

In essence, the most captivating aspect of Gen Z's engagement with space tourism is the blend of idealism, technological savvy, and a forward-looking mindset. Their collective imagination is propelling discussions about the future of human exploration, not just as a distant dream but as a tangible and achievable reality within their lifetime. As they actively contribute to shaping the narrative around space tourism, Gen Z exemplifies a generation that sees the cosmos as both a playground for adventure and a canvas for responsible innovation.

The Financial Literacy

Gen Z is navigating the landscape of financial literacy with a distinctive reliance on technology, leveraging a variety of digital resources to enhance their understanding of personal finance. The integration of technology into their financial education is a testament to this generation's comfort with digital tools and their proactive approach to acquiring financial knowledge.

Apps play a pivotal role in Gen Z's financial journey. Mobile applications like Robinhood, Cash App, and Venmo provide them with firsthand experience in budgeting, investing, and managing transactions. The simplicity and accessibility of these apps resonate with Gen Z's preference for user-friendly interfaces.

Educational platforms and websites are instrumental in providing structured financial lessons. Resources such as Investopedia, Khan Academy, and dedicated personal finance apps deliver interactive tutorials, breaking down complex financial concepts into digestible content. Gen Z embraces the flexibility of online learning, allowing them to acquire financial literacy at their own pace.

Social media platforms serve not only as entertainment but also as hubs for financial advice. Influencers on TikTok, Instagram, and YouTube share insights into budgeting hacks, investment strategies, and practical tips for building credit. The bite-sized, engaging nature of these platforms aligns with Gen Z's short attention spans and preference for quick, actionable information.

The rise of cryptocurrency has also captured the curiosity of Gen Z. Many in this generation are exploring the intricacies of blockchain technology, decentralized finance (DeFi), and various cryptocurrencies as part of their financial education. The decentralized and tech-forward nature of the crypto space resonates with their digital-first mindset.

Furthermore, online courses and webinars cater to Gen Z's desire for structured learning experiences. Platforms like Coursera and Udemy offer courses covering diverse financial topics, empowering individuals to delve into subjects such as investing, financial planning, and economic principles.

In essence, Gen Z's financial literacy journey is intertwined with technology, with a multifaceted approach that incorporates apps, educational platforms, social media, and emerging financial technologies. This generation's proactive use of digital tools reflects a dynamic and adaptive approach to financial education, positioning them to navigate the complexities of personal finance in an increasingly digital world.

www.ingramcontent.com/pod-product-compliance
Lightning Source LLC
LaVergne TN
LVHW091050150826
845673LV00002B/530

* 9 7 9 8 8 9 2 3 3 8 5 4 7 *